Uwe Wohlfahrt

IT Investment Evaluation

Uwe Wohlfahrt

IT Investment Evaluation

A Suitability Analysis
of Financial Evaluation Measures

VDM Verlag Dr. Müller

Bibliographic information by the German National Library: The German National Library li‌
this publication at the German National Bibliography; detailed bibliographic information i‌
available on the Internet at http://dnb.d-nb.de.

Copyright © 2006 VDM Verlag Dr. Müller e. K. und Lizenzgeber
All rights reserved. Saarbrücken 2006
Contact: info@vdm-buchverlag.de
Cover image: www.photocase.de
Produced by: Lightning Source Inc., La Vergne, Tennessee/USA
         Lightning Source UK Ltd., Milton Keynes, UK

Bibliografische Information der Deutschen Nationalbibliothek: Die Deutsche
Nationalbibliothek verzeichnet diese Publikation in der Deutschen Nationalbibliografie;
detaillierte bibliografische Daten sind im Internet über http://dnb.d-nb.de abrufbar.

Copyright © 2006 VDM Verlag Dr. Müller e. K. und Lizenzgeber
Alle Rechte vorbehalten. Saarbrücken 2006
Kontakt: info@vdm-buchverlag.de
Coverbild: www.photocase.de
Herstellung: Lightning Source Inc., La Vergne, Tennessee/USA
         Lightning Source UK Ltd., Milton Keynes, UK

ISBN-10: 3-86550-454-X
ISBN-13: 978-3-86550-454-8

Contents

List of Figures

List of Tables

Abbreviations

CEO	Chief Executive Officer
Cf.	Confer
CFO	Chief Financial Officer
CFROI	Cash Flow Return On Investment
CIO	Chief Information Officer
CRM	Customer Relationship Management
CTO	Chief Technical Officer
DCF	Discounted Cash Flow
e.g.	For example
EBIT	Earnings Before Interest and Taxes
EDW	Enterprise Data Warehouse
ERP	Enterprise Resource Planning
Etc.	Et cetera
EVA	Economic Value Added
GCF	Gross-Cash-Flow
GIB	Gross-Investment-Basis
HGB	Handelsgesetzbuch
IAS	International Accounting Standards
IRR	Internal Rate of Return
IS	Information Systems
IT	Information Technology
MIRR	Modified Internal Rate of Return
MVA	Market Value Added
NOA	Net Operating Assets
NOPAT	Net Operating Profit After Taxes
NPV	Net Present Value
NV	Net Value of non-depreciatable assets
R&D	Research and Development
ROA	Return On Asset
ROE	Return On Equity
ROI	Return On Investment
ROIT	Return On Information Technology
ROM	Return On Management
SCM	Supply Chain Management
TCO	Total Cost of Ownership
US-GAAP	United States - Generally Accepted Accounting Principles
WACC	Weighted Average Cost of Capital
w-lan	wireless-local area network

1. Introduction

1.1 Problem formulation

Investments in IT seem to go without saying. IT, which consists of computer hardware, software, telecommunications and data networks and all support required to operate these systems, is said to enhance organizational capabilities, resulting in improved product quality and variety, increased customer satisfaction and hence contributing to sales increases. IT should further enable rationalization of processes within companies and open up new business opportunities and markets by changing fundamental firm practises, to name only a few expectations that arise from IT investments. Most executives agree that "investing in the development of an IT infrastructure is critical to being competitive in practically any industrial or consumer market anywhere"[1]. But at the same time they cannot even specify the benefits of these investments or do not know how to quantify them. Improvements, enabled by IT, are often not reflected in improved financial performance or productivity growth. The shortfall of evidence of IT–enabled increases in business productivity is entitled as the "productivity paradox"[2], introduced by Brynjolfsson and later solved by Brynjolfsson and Hitt and other researchers.

Because companies can no longer afford to make extensive technology purchases without understanding the return of those investments, each project has to be weighed to determine whether it contributes strategic value to a company or not. Those who want to sell their IT products, like technology solution providers or consultants, are usually confronted with the demands of their clients for suitable evidence of IT benefits that would justify the expenses.

The most common and accepted measure to justify investments is the return on investment (ROI), which is not different for investments in IT. Nevertheless, it is dubious if such a financial measure and other metrics can reflect intangible benefits, long-term strategic advantages and other benefits that are enabled by IT investments.

---

[1] Smith David et al. (2002), p. 101.
[2] For detailed information on the productivity paradox please refer to Brynjolfsson (1993) and Brynjolfsson and Hitt (1993).

1.2 Purpose of this work

The main question to be answered by this book is: How suitable are financial evaluation methods to evaluate IT investments? In the intention to answer the question of the correct measures for IT investment evaluation several questions occur. These are:

- Does a single evaluation measure exist that is generally "the best" for IT investment appraisal?
- Are financial performance measures capable of evaluating all aspects that arise from IT investments?
- Does valuating IT investments only by financial performance measures prevent them from being carried out?
- How can one know if and when payoff from previous or future IT investments will be realized?

These questions can only be answered if it is possible to evaluate IT investments correctly. For a proper examination of the correct measurement concept it is necessary to highlight the characteristics of evaluation measures as well as of IT investments.

1.3 Course of action

This work is structured as follows. Adjacent to the introduction, the second chapter will highlight the differences between "usual" investments and IT investments and deal with the nature of IT investments. In the third chapter this work will examine the different evaluation methods used in financial accounting and elaborate if these methods can meet the requirements that arise from IT. This chapter will begin with the establishment of a framework by which the different methods are analyzed and close with an overview of the gained results. Afterwards the status quo of IT investment evaluation will be shown, which aims at answering the question if IT investment evaluation in practise is done properly and whether there are more reasonable evaluation methods or not. The main focus of this fourth chapter will be the analysis of discovered problems and their solutions. The final chapter will summarize the conclusions gained in the previous analysis.

2 Characteristics of IT investments

In order to accomplish a proper analysis of IT investment evaluation measures one has to be aware of the specific characteristics of these investments in contrast to common capital investments. Different characteristics require different methods of evaluation. Therefore, this chapter will point out these features in preparation for the following chapter that will examine the suitability of each financial measure for IT investment evaluation.

2.1 Cost structure

In the context of information technology, one can speak of the "cost iceberg" because "IT costs are scattered across many budgets and ... only 20% of them are clearly visible"[3]. Information Technology consists of hardware and software components which have to be evaluated differently. The hardware components range from desktop computers and monitors over servers to infrastructure components, such as cabling, router, switches or w-lan components. Besides these obvious costs, other cost drivers exist that are correlated with the implementation and usage of IT systems. These involve amongst others, salaries for IT consultants and experts who conduct implementation processes, ensure ongoing support after the implementation and train personnel in the use of the new technology. Direct costs are costs of development and implementation of the applications systems including all acquisition costs and transpositions.[4] Ongoing costs are such as support, maintenance, costs for consumable material, occupancy costs, taxes and insurance costs, hire and capital costs, salaries and power consumption.[5]

Characteristical for many IT investments are "hidden costs of information technology, such as complementary organizational investments required to realize the benefits of IT"[6]. These hidden costs are also called indirect, tacit or soft costs. Table 1 should give an overview of possible costs of IT investments.

---

[3] Keen in Devaraj and Kohli (2002), Foreword XIV.
[4] Cf. Stahlknecht and Hasenkamp (2002), p. 252.
[5] Cf. Schwarze (2000), p. 200.
[6] Brynjolfsson and Yang (1996), p. 21.

All these costs that occur at an IT project can be measured ex-post but useful in the case of deciding for or against an IT investment would they be at an ex-ante view. And this is the actual problem, forecasting future costs and integrating them into calculations, weighted with their probabilities of occurrence. For instance, the costs for implantation and installation could rise unexpectedly when problems occur, which could not be predicted, time schedules could be exceeded, the implemented system could show failures that lead to long downtimes and many more. A good way to decrease the inaccuracy of the estimations on the costs factors is to rely on past similar projects whose costs are ex-post known. However, a complete elimination of the involved uncertainties cannot be achieved.

Direct costs	Indirect costs
Acquisition costs	Support
Hardware	Administration
Software	Training
Installation / Upgrade	Maintenance
Implementation	Downtime
	Power Consumption
	Evaluation
	Futz
	Auditing
	Complementary Organizational Investments

Table 1: IT investment costs; Source: own illustration.

Acquisition costs usually constitute only about 20 percent of the overall costs, while the rest lies in ongoing costs such as installation, implementation, support, downtime, training and maintenance.[7] Gormely et al. (1998) presented the shares of several types of costs for the example of an ERP Suite. The most remarkable information from this example is that the implementation consumes nearly half of the overall start-up costs and that costs for hardware components play only a meagre role.[8] Under

---

[7] Cf. Smith David et al. (2003), pp. 102-103.
[8] Cf. Gormely et al. (1998), cited in Brynjolfsson and Yang (1999), p.42.

this circumstance, it is a matter of common knowledge that assigning specific expenses to cost factors is a difficult task. Therefore, the shares can vary in different studies but can still provide us with useful round figures on cost allocation. For instance, compensations for external consultants are assigned to deployment costs in this example but could also be expensed as software service purchase accounts.[9] On the other hand, internal and external consultants are not only involved in deployment or implementation but also take part in redesigning information flows or business processes.[10] Significant in this circumstance is the fact that the total annual ongoing costs of such an ERP suite are about 45% of the total start-up costs.[11]

A complete prediction of IT costs in general is nearly impossible due to the rapid changes in input costs provoked by the appearance of new substituting technologies and the usage of insufficient valuation measures for estimating project expenses.

2.2 Intangibility

Living in the "information age" and considering the growth in communication and information technologies over the last decade, it is hardly deniable that the share of intangible assets to total assets in today's modern firms is remarkably higher than in the past.

But what actually are intangibles? Intangible is usually defined as "incapable of being perceived by senses" or "incapable of being realized or defined". Definitions for intangible assets are numerous. They are "characterized by a lack of physical substance" or "Other than tangible or financial". The International Accounting Standard (IAS 38) defines an intangible asset as "an identifiable nonmonetary asset without physical substance"[12] that has to follow three criteria:

- the asset meets the definition of an intangible asset and is thus identifiable,
- is controlled by the entity and

---

[9] Cf. Brynjolfsson and Yang (1999), p. 28.

[10] Cf. Brynjolfsson and Yang (1999), pp. 28-29.

[11] Cf. Gormely et al. (1998), cited in Brynjolfsson and Yang (1999), p. 42.

[12] Deloitte (2005).

- future economic benefits and reduced costs that are attributable to the asset will flow to the entity.[13]

A firm can possess a multitude of intangible assets such as copyrights, patents, know-how, strong customer relationships, improved workflow, brand names and many more.[14] The outcome of in-house development of software for instance is difficult to evaluate. After German HGB these self-developed intangible assets cannot be shown in the balance sheet and the US-American US-GAAP requires certain parts of the costs of developing software for internal use to be capitalized under certain conditions. This not or partly allowed activation of certain intangible assets is of interest, when considering that the income-share of software can be about 70 percent of that of the hardware and up to 50 percent of software spending is allocated to in-house development depending on the examined industry sector.[15] Only the IAS allows the complete consideration of self-developed software. But intangibles can still be measured because "the financial market evaluation of firms can be used to estimate the intangible costs and benefits of computer capital"[16]. An announcement of large-scale investment in IT of any stock market listed company is often correlated with a significant increase in stock market valuation. Some researchers see "intangible resources as the main drivers for the sustainability of performance differences across firms"[17]. Still, remembering the "Internet Bubble Burst" in 2000, it is questionable to what extend one should trust in stock market values or stock market analysts.

Concentrating on firm level data, instead on industry data or that of a whole economy, it should be possible to successfully link an increase in a firm's revenue to an increase in intangible assets such as better quality or convenience, although this value could not be directly observed.[18] Using the original q-theory[19] of investment, which is analyzed in detail in chapter 3.2.7, the estimated average value of q for computer hardware, is 10, which is quite

---

[13] Cf. Deloitte (2005).
[14] Cf. Van Grembergen (2001), p. 160.
[15] Cf. Brynjolfsson and Yang (1999), pp. 27-28.
[16] Brynjolfsson and Yang (1999), p. 1.
[17] Villalonga (2004), p. 206.
[18] Cf. Brynjolfsson and Hitt (1998), pp. 5-6.
[19] The q-theory provides a ratio of a firm's market value to a firm's book value. The q value shows, if one should invest further into that capital. If q is greater than one, further investment in capital by the firm will be profitable. If q is less than one, further investment will not be profitable.

high in comparison to the value of 1 for reproducible assets.[20] Brynjolfsson and Yang (1999) argue, that the source of these high valuations are computer related intangible assets, such as capitalized adjustment costs, software, new business practises and other complementary organizational innovations.[21] Brynjolfsson and Hitt (1998) presented an analysis that suggested that a 1 dollar change in IT capital is associated with a change of 10 dollars in market evaluation of such firms.

Asking users of newly adopted IT, e.g. a CRM system, about the benefits of the new software, a common answer may be that they have the feeling that customer satisfaction has increased. In order to transfer such soft factors into hard factors, it would be necessary to express it in a mathematical formula, e.g. that an x percent better customer satisfaction leads to a y percent increase in total revenue.[22] But such formulas simply do not exist for now.

2.3 Impact on organizational structures

Brynjolfsson and Hitt (1998) stated that "the greatest benefits of computers appear to be realized when computer investment is coupled with other complementary investments; new strategies, new business processes and new organizations all appear to be important in realizing the maximum benefit in IT"[23]. This implies that possessing technology alone does not create benefits. Creating "real value" from IT requires efficient management processes.[24] Carrying out extensive changes, much effort has to be brought up, but at the end the possible benefits should be more than adequate.

Studies further found out that benefits due to organizational changes can barely be measured for the short-term but in the long-term computer investments contribute 2 to 8 times more to output growth.[25] One reason for the lag between investment outlays and recoupment of these outlays is that "the organiza-

---

[20] Cf. Brynjolfsson and Yang (1999), p. 3.

[21] Cf. Brynjolfsson and Yang (1999), p. 3.

[22] Cf. Selchert (2004), pp. 28-29.

[23] Brynjolfsson and Hitt (1998), p. 3.

[24] Cf. Van der Zee (2002), p. 4.

[25] Cf. Brynjolfsson and Hitt (2000), p. 25.

tional factors that unlock the value of IT are costly and time consuming"[26].

Pointing out the sequence that investment in IT should be followed by complementary investments and organizational changes in order to realize the "real value of IT", we should not conceal the reverse sequence. Namely, IT investments are necessarily undertaken out of the need for structural changes in organizations caused by general changes in the economy, increased diffusion of IT into workplace and new management trends such as business process redesign.[27]

However, Brynjolfsson and Hitt (1998) also pointed out that changing a whole company in its core business processes, management infrastructure, replacing staff and changing fundamental firm practises is time consuming, risky and costly.[28] Projects of such magnitude are always confronted with difficulties and failures of change, so that executives, that are generally pleased with their old possibly not optimal but well know organizational structures, may be reluctant deciding for such fundamental changes.[29] But at the same time, these costly and risky projects "create barriers for competitors seeking to match the investment"[30]. Managers are also advised not to conduct half-hearted IT investments, neglecting a redesigning of management processes, because this could lead to low administrative productivity.[31]

A major advantage of the impact of IT on organizational structures can be that it may open up completely new business opportunities. Investments in integrated ERP and CRM systems may give companies the ability to explore new distribution channels, to reach new customer markets or to produce products of better quality and variety or even new products.

A factor that should not be ignored is the human factor. People have to cope with the information technology that should support them at their work. The optimal case would be an IT that is tailored to the needs of its users. If that is not the case, people tend to meet new systems with more or less resistance. Besides the fact that change in general can be seen negatively by some

---

[26] Brynjolfsson and Hitt (1998), p. 7.
[27] Cf. Brynjolfsson and Hitt (1998), p. 8.
[28] Cf. Brynjolfsson and Hitt (1998), p. 9.
[29] Brynjolfsson and Hitt (1998), p. 9.
[30] Brynjolfsson and Yang (1999), p. 30.
[31] Cf. Rai et al. (1997), p. 97.

people, adjusting to new technology is always an additional burden to users. Nevertheless, because of increased requirements for integration of information systems (IS) with business operations, trained personnel has become a critical component of IS capabilities.[32] Training costs and salaries can constitute a high fraction of IS budgets but these expenses are reflected in increased firm output and labor productivity.[33]

Even if everybody is aware of the benefits that accompany complementary investments and organizational changes, the question of a proper measurement of these values remains unanswered. Balance sheets do not include these values and most traditional evaluation measures just as little. Is the valuation of a company on the stock market value again, as it could be seen in chapter 2.2, the only way to pay respect to this aspect of IT investments?

2.4 Uncertainty

Uncertainty in the context of IT investments exists towards:
- Success of the implementation / adoption.
- Costs for support, downtime and maintenance of the implemented IT.
- Future paybacks, intangible (e.g. customer satisfaction) as well as tangible (e.g. cash flows) ones.
- Future business opportunities provided by the new IT.

The implementation or adoption of a new technology into an existing IT infrastructure is easier said than done. Investment projects can fail as a result of insufficient consultations of all involved parties or an underestimation of the complexity of such projects. Expert know-how and consulting is necessary to successfully meet those challenges.

As mentioned before, many costs that emerge during an IT project can be valued in advance, but there is still a certain degree of uncertainty in predicting costs. The computer market is rapidly changing concerning the quality and functional range of hardware and software. The time period in which computer components become obsolete decreases more and more. The quality of computer components is also not guaranteed and uncertainty arises towards accident sensitivity of a new technology, which can cause

---

[32] Cf. Rai et al. (1997), p. 95.
[33] Cf. Rai et al. (1997), p. 95.

high support costs and long downtimes. Uncertainty concerning the benefits of IT investments is even higher. Pronouncing that the new IT will lead to better product quality and hence to a higher demand and revenue is done easily, but providing exact numbers for this prediction is a rather difficult task.

3 Evaluation measures and their suitability for IT investment evaluation

3.1 Analysis framework

Some studies restrain themselves on analyzing only a particular type of IT investments, e.g. development, acquisition, infrastructure, prototyping or technology-as-product investments. The following analysis will try to analyze evaluation measures on their suitability for evaluating IT investments of any kind and whole companies that have undergone investments in IT or themselves develop and sell IT products. Therefore, each measure is presented in its theoretical background with regard to the particular benefits and shortcomings. Afterwards they are analyzed towards their suitability for IT investment evaluation with especially considering the characteristics that all these investments have in common, presented in the previous chapter and listed in the following table.

IT Investment Characteristics	
Cost structure	Direct costs
	Indirect costs
Intangibility	Intangible assets
Impact on organizational structures	Long-term benefits
	New business opportunities
	Organizational changes
Uncertainty	Benefits uncertainty
	Costs uncertainty

Table 2: IT investment characteristics; Source: own illustration.

The questions concerning each financial evaluation measure that this chapter tries to answer are:
1. Are all costs, direct and indirect, included in the particular measure?
2. Are intangible assets included and if so, to what extent?
3. Is the impact of IT investments on organizational structures taken into account? This includes complementary investments, organizational changes, long-term benefits and new business opportunities.

4. Do the measures pay regard to uncertainty towards costs and benefits?

3.2 Evaluation measures analysis

3.2.1 Amortization / Payback

3.2.1.1 Theoretical foundation

The payback period and the amortization time describe the same issue, which is the "time required for the project's expected after-tax incremental cash flow to repay the entire initial investment in the project"[34]. The following example visualizes this concept:[35]

Periods	0	1	2	3
Project A	-600	300	300	100
Project B	-600	250	250	250

Table 3: Amortization example; Source: In the style of Drukarczyk (2003), p. 11.

Project A has an amortization time of 2 periods because the initial investment of 600 is recouped by a surplus of 300 for the next 2 periods, while the amortization time of project B is 3 periods. Judging investments by the amortization time, project A has to be chosen due to its faster recoupment.

But this static concept has two shortcomings:
- It does not consider the time after the specific amortization period.
- It does not consider the costs of deployed capital.

The effects of these shortcomings can best be explained with an example. Under the assumption that money can be lend at an interest rate of 10 percent, the gross capital value[36] of the previous amortization example will be calculated:

---

[34] Broyles (2003), p. 87.
[35] The following after Drukarczyk (2003), pp. 11-15.
[36] The gross capital value constitutes the specific amount that has to be invested on the capital market at an interest rate i in period 0, in order to achieve the exact receipt of payment, which is generated by the investment project.

$$\text{Gross Capital Value of Project A} = \frac{300}{1,1^1} + \frac{300}{1,1^2} + \frac{100}{1,1^3} = 595,79$$

$$\text{Gross Capital Value of Project B} = \frac{250}{1,1^1} + \frac{250}{1,1^2} + \frac{250}{1,1^3} = 621,71.$$

As these results show, Project A, which has to be chosen after the amortization method, should not be chosen because it does not earn the interest rate of 10 percent that could be earned by alternatively investing the initial 600 on the capital market. Now project B will be preferred, because 621,71 had to be paid on the capital market to achieve the same receipt payments when only 600 are needed for the investment project, although its amortization time is inferior to project A.

The analysis of payback period and amortization time respectively done by Drukarczyk (2003) seems plausible. But there are other methods and formulae besides the standard definition of calculating it. A frequently used modified formula is:

$$\text{Payback Period} = \frac{\text{The Costs of Project / Investment}}{\text{Annual Cash Flows}}.$$

A calculation of the payback period of the previous example, using this equation, results into contrary findings:

$$\text{Payback Period of Project A} = \frac{600}{\left(\dfrac{300 + 300 + 100}{3}\right)} = 2.57$$

$$\text{Payback Period of Project B} = \frac{600}{\left(\dfrac{250 + 250 + 250}{3}\right)} = 2.40$$

This time, project B has to be chosen due to its shorter recoupment, contrary to the first results after Drukarczyk (2003). The formula simply includes the divisibility of the underlying periods. However, the two shortcomings still exist.

The following modified payback formula even includes the costs of capital by calculating the net present value (NPV) of the savings additional to an annual calculation:

$$Payback\ Period = \frac{Initial\ Investment}{\left(\dfrac{NPV\ of\ Savings}{Years_n} \right)}.$$

Thereby, one shortcoming that was mentioned previously is disposed.

3.2.1.2 Suitability analysis

The amortization time should only be computed for investment projects of low complexity, because it is necessary to determine the exact returns and costs of an investment. As pointed out in chapter 2, IT investments can be very complex and consist of tangible and intangible costs and benefits which alone would be a reason not to use the amortization time for these kinds of investments. In addition the characteristic of many IT investments that there is a considerable time lag between the initial investment and its recoupment, does affect the explanatory power of this measure. Using the amortization method on IT investments and comparing the result with those of other capital investments would lead to a discrimination of IT investments, due to the favouritism of investments with fast recoupments. Amortization time alone is usually not meaningful enough and should be accompanied by other performance measures. It does not take any intangibles, impacts on organizational structure or uncertainties into account. Only initial investment costs are taken into consideration and ongoing costs are ignored. Using a modified amortization formula does not affect any of these disadvantages. A comparison of payback periods done by different companies for similar projects is only recommendable when all agree on using the same formula.

However, comparing two IT investment projects with similar characteristics can provide decision makers with significant information and enable them to make the right decisions. Generally, the amortization method can be a useful measure for evaluating projects of low complexity and fast recoupment and can provide managers with information about a project's efficiency.

3.2.2   Return on investment / equity / assets

3.2.2.1   Theoretical foundation

The Return on Investment (ROI) is probably the most popular and most accepted financial performance measure. One reason for this circumstance may be its simplicity and tangibility, which makes it a good argument at every consideration about possible investments. It was first introduced in 1912 by the CFO of DuPont, Donaldson Brown.[37] The basic ROI is simply the income of a certain year, subtracted of the taxes, divided by the average book value of assets of the same year:

$$ROI = \frac{\text{Net income}}{\text{Book value of assets}} \quad \text{or}$$

$$ROI = \frac{\text{Net income} + \text{Interest}\,(1 - \text{Tax rate})}{\text{Book value of assets}}.$$

The first equation contains a bias caused by different methods of financing.[38] The return on investment is higher at equity financing than at dept financing. Therefore the second equation is often used to avoid this bias. Another problem is the limitation to a single period that can partly be evaded by computing an average ROI for several periods.

Comparing ROI and discounted cash flow (DCF), Ezra Solomon and others came to the conclusion that the "ROI is not an accurate or reliable estimate of the DCF return"[39]. Assuming a known DCF return, "ROI sometimes underestimates, but more often overstates, the DCF rate"[40]. Solomon identified four factors that influence the extent to which ROI overstates the economic or DCF return:[41]

- "*Length of project life*. The longer the project life, the greater the overstatement". Reason: Profits will be realized, when assets are already depreciated.

---

[37] Cf. Ewert and Wagenhofer (2003), p. 552.
[38] The following theoretical foundation of ROI after Rappaport (1998), pp. 23-29.
[39] Rappaport (1998), p. 23.
[40] Rappaport (1998), p. 23.
[41] The following influence factors are cited after Rappaport (1998), p. 23.

- *"Capitalization policy.* The smaller the fraction of total investment capitalized on the books, the greater the overstatement".
- *"The rate at which depreciation is taken on the book assets.* The faster the depreciation, the higher the ROI". Reason: Profits will be realized, when assets are already depreciated.
- *"The lag between investment outlays and recoupment of these outlays from cash flows.* The greater the lag, the greater the degree of overstatement". Reason: no discounting.

Rappaport (1998) also dealt with general shortcomings of ROI and found three fundamental reasons why the use of ROI as an evaluation measure at the business unit or corporate level can lead to misallocation of resources and executive misjudgments. The first is, that comparing two companies with identical strategies and expectations, the one company with the larger beginning investment base will have lower ROIs during the planning period, while at the same time the DCF return of the two companies are identical.

Secondly, the ROI does not take the post planning residual value of the business unit or company into account. By doing so, it ignores up to 50 percent of a company's market value. Although actions that aim at strengthening the company's long-term strategic position such as increased spending in product development, marketing or extended production capacity increases value, the ROI of such companies may decline over the following years. The conversed strategy of minimizing investments in fixed capital and freeing up working capital, the so called "Harvesting Strategy", will generate higher ROIs while the residual value declines and therefore the long-term market position can be weakened.

At the third and last shortcoming of ROI, Rappaport (1998) examines the effects of financing policy on ROI. Basis for the following examination is an optimal capital structure (proportion of dept to equity) of the considered company, which is characterized by a minimized weighted average cost of capital (WACC). Miles and Ezzell (1980) find the WACC to be an appropriate discount rate for a one year project life as well as level perpetual project cash flows.[42] It is a calculation of a firm's cost of capital that weights all capital sources, equity and dept, proportionately. A

---

[42] Cf. Miles and Ezzell (1980), p. 720.

change of that capital structure would result in an increased WACC and reduce the value of the firm. [43] The effect of an increased or decreased dept on ROI is shortly summarized as follows. The ROI before interest is not affected by financing policy while the shareholder value, therefore also the WACC, decreases whenever the firm moves away from the optimal dept. But a less than optimal dept leads to an increase of the ROI after interest, although a less than optimal dept means that the value of the firm decreases.

A to the ROI related ratio is the return on equity (ROE) ,which is defined as the net income divided by the book value of shareholders equity:

$$ROE = \frac{\text{Net income}}{\text{Book value of shareholders' equity}}.$$

"Profitability as measured by Return on Equity (ROE) ... provides an alternative measure of how effectively a firm has utilized its financial capital"[44]. While ROI is mostly used at the business unit or divisional level, ROE is preferred by investors at the corporate level.[45] As the ROE is similar to the ROI, it shares the same shortcomings. Rappaport judges the ROE to be an even less reliable measure for corporate performance than it used to be in the past. He points out that, unlike in the mid-1990s where only a few companies could join the so called "20 percent club"[46], it has become more and more common to exceed this ratio. Rappaport (1998) identified three reasons for this development: "improved profit margins, increased assets turnover, or increased leverage defined as assets divided by stockholders' equity"[47].

Another to the ROI and ROE related ratio is the return on assets (ROA). "Profitability as measured by Return on Assets (ROA) ... measures how effectively a firm has utilized its existing physical

---

[43] For more detailed information on WACC please refer to Miles and Ezzell (1980).
[44] Hit and Brynjolfsson (1994), p. 10.
[45] The following after Rappaport (1998), pp. 29-31.
[46] The "20 percent club" indicates that all firms in that club have a ROE ratio of 20 percent.
[47] Rappaport (1998), p. 30

capital to earn income"[48]. It is usually defined as the profit margin multiplied by the turnover of the underlying assets:

$$ROA = Profit\ margin \times Asset\ turnover$$

while asset turnover is computed as follows:

$$Asset\ turnover = \frac{total\ asset\ at\ the\ BOP + total\ asset\ at\ the\ EOP}{2}$$

where BOP is the beginning of period and EOP is the end of period. The ROA can either be calculated as net or gross ROA, by using the net profit margin or gross profit margin. At an alternative ROA formula the net income is divided by the average assets for the period:

$$ROA = \frac{Net\ income}{Average\ assets\ for\ the\ period}.$$

A use of this formula in gross values would lead to the following formula:

$$Gross\ ROA = \frac{EBIT}{Average\ assets\ for\ the\ period}$$

where EBIT are the earnings before interest and taxes.

The close relation between ROE and ROA is reflected by the following formula:

$$ROE = ROA(net) \times Equity\ multiplier.$$

3.2.2.2   Suitability analysis

Considering the previously mentioned factors for an overstatement of ROI towards DCF with regard to IT investments, the first and fourths factors are of interest. As pointed out in chapter 2, IT investments can have a *long project life* due to the complexity concerning the phase of implementing a new system in an existing, mostly inadequate IT infrastructure, training of personnel in the use of the new systems and many others factors. The *lag*

---

[48] Hit and Brynjolfsson (1994), p. 10.

*between investment outlays and recoupments of these outlays
from cash flows* can also be considerably, possibly there is no
measurable recoupment at all. The other two influence factors can
also concern IT investments, but are not especially characteristic
for these. This implies that an ROI used at IT investments would
most probably overstate the DCF rate.

Concerning the three general shortcomings on ROI, found by
Rappaport, the first two of them regard IT investments. The first
describes that companies with larger beginning investment bases
have lower ROIs. Hence, a company that undertakes higher investments in IT in order to ensure its future competitiveness or to
achieve other goals, which would usually be regarded positively,
will have lower ROIs. The second shortcoming also describes lower
ROIs, this time well-founded by not considering the post planning
residual value. As the post planning residual value is often an
important benefit of IT investments, this shortcoming fully applies
to them.

Considering the whole ROI analysis by Rappaport, it is not
astonishing that it is his opinion that the "ROI performance during
the planning period alone is not a reliable basis for estimating
economic return"[49]. Other researchers found similar shortcomings
of this concept. Ewert and Wagenhofer (2003) describe in detail
how the use of ROI can lead to an under- as well as overstatement
of investment projects.[50]

In addition to the analysis of the basic ROI metric, a different
approach of ROI calculation for an e-commerce project done by
Mogollon and Raisinghani (2004) will follow.[51] The ROI for this
project is computed by dividing the return, calculated of all
savings and any monetary measurable unit generated by the project in time, by the costs and any monetary unit required to plan,
execute and complete the project in time:

$$ROI = \frac{Project\ Return}{Cost\ to\ Implement\ the\ Project}.$$

This equation again seems to be very simple, but the problem
in practise is the determination of what constitutes the total

---

[49] Rappaport (1998), p. 28.
[50] Cf. Ewert and Wagenhofer (2003), pp. 550-558.
[51] The following ROI calculation for an e-commerce project after Mogollon and
     Raisinghani (2004), pp. 187-197.

return and costs of a project. Besides an easy determination of tangible costs and benefits, intangible components are especially difficult to determine. Therefore, Mogollon and Raisinghani (2004) concentrated in the following two steps on analyzing the enumerator and denominator of this equation. The enumerator (Project Return) can be determined by subtracting the costs that incur with the new process from the costs that incurred with the former process before implementation of the new technology and adding "other benefits" which consist of intangible benefits or so called "soft benefits", e.g. customer satisfaction, improved employee moral and others. The now advanced ROI formula is as follows:

$$ROI = \frac{\text{Current Process Cost} - \text{New Process Cost} + \text{Other Benefits}}{\text{Cost to Implement the Project}}.$$

By calculating changes in process costs, this approach takes the effects of organizational changes into account.

Focusing on the denominator (Cost to Implement the Project), it can be determined by costs for the initial investment and operating and maintenance costs during the use of the technology. This includes a time factor in the equation and Mogollon and Raisinghani recommend a time period of three years, due to the rapid change in e-commerce technologies. The final ROI equation can be written as:

$$ROI = \frac{(\text{Curr. Proc. Cost} - \text{New Proc. Cost} + \text{Other Benefits}) \text{ per year} \times 3 \text{ years}}{\text{Initial Investment} + (\text{Operation and Maintanance per year}) \times 3 \text{ years}}$$

Using the net present value (NPV) to calculate the costs and benefits, the ROI formula is as follows:

$$ROI = \frac{\sum_1^n PV\left[(\text{Curr. Proc. Cost} - \text{New Proc. Cost} + \text{Other Benefits}) \text{ per year}\right]}{\sum_1^n PV\left[\text{Initial Investment} + (\text{Operating and Maintanance per year})\right]}$$

The "Other Benefits" included in the equations are difficult to quantify but methods have been developed, which try to solve this problem. "ROI calculator tools" are one of these methods. Mogollon and Raisinghani (2004) describe how these work on a hypothetical example. The calculators can include intangible benefits such as customer satisfaction, customer and employee retention, decreased time to market, reduced sales outstanding and web improvement.[52] In the following, this will be illustrated on the example of customer retention. The basis is a company that tries to reduce the losing of 10 percent of its customers a year to 4 percent by implementing a CRM application. The first step is to group the customers into profitability segments. Secondly, it should be determined what percentage, of the 10 percent the company is losing, is in each profitability segment:[53]

$$\text{Customer Lost} = \text{number of cust.} \times \text{total \% of lost cust.} \times \text{\%per segment}$$
$$\text{Re tained Cust.} = \text{number of cust.} \times \text{\% goal for retined cust.} \times \text{\%per segment}$$

Then, the profits that the company will gain by customer retaining should be calculated:

$$\text{Gained Pr ofits} = \text{Number of Re tined Cust.} \times \text{Pr ofit per segment}$$

Summarizing the resulting gained profits of all customer segments provides the profit gained by implementing a CRM application. Similar calculations can be done for other intangible benefits.

After being confronted with so many shortcomings of the basic ROI previously, it may be of interest seeing if these shortcomings also apply to the adjusted ROI after Mogollon and Raisinghani. The following shortcomings do not or only partly apply to their approach.

The limitation of the basic ROI to a single period, that can only partly be solved by calculating an average ROI for several periods, does not apply to their approach. The aspect of longer project life cycles is included in their equations by computing the costs and benefits per year and discounting it to the present time.

The allegation that the ROI does not take the post planning residual value into account, also does not apply for their approach. It includes "Other Benefits" and therefore intangible benefits that occur mostly in the post planning period.

The longer the project life, the greater the overstatement of ROI towards DCF return. The reason is that profits will be realized, when assets are already depreciated. The Mogollon and

---

[52] Cf. Mogollon and Raisinghani (2004), p. 203.
[53] The following after Mogollon and Raisinghani (2004), pp. 205-211.

Raisinghani approach assumes that e-commerce applications have a life cycle of three years, during which they realize their benefits and will then be replaced by new applications. Therefore, this reason for an overstatement does not apply.

The greater the lag between investment outlays and recoupment of these outlays from cash flows the greater the degree of overstatement. This does only occur when the ROI is calculated for a single period and a correlation between initial investment and later generated cash flows does not exist. The e-commerce adjusted ROI considers the time factor and is not affect-ted by this overstatement effect.

Although the two approaches are based on different assumptions, the conclusion that the e-commerce adjusted ROI can eliminate some shortcomings of the basic ROI can be made. All other shortcomings, benefits and disadvantages do also apply to this approach. In the end, the basic ROI does not take all IT investment characteristics into account but its comparability with ROIs of other companies is possible. The adjusted ROI is a tool for management accounting and not for financial reporting, and thus underlies a high degree of arbitrariness. Every firm can adjust the ROI to its specific needs and characteristics. Therefore, a compa-rison between adjusted ROIs of two or more companies or their investment projects is not reasonable. But it can be adjusted according to the existing circumstances of a firm's projects and Mogollon and Raisinghani have shown how this can be realized. In doing so, an adjusted ROI can take some IT investment Charac-teristics into account. These are intangible costs and benefits and organizational changes. Uncertainties, business opportunities and long-term benefits are unfortunately not considered.

A major problem with ROI as well as ROE occurs when it comes to comparing knowledge-based companies such as software-developing companies with those companies investing principally in fixed assets.[54] Companies that invest mainly in intan-gibles such as information, training and research, have a lower capitalization for accounting purposes and thus a lower ROI and ROE.

A connection between ROE and IT investments may exist when the deployed shareholder equity is used to conduct these investments. Therefore, it is important for shareholders to know if

---

[54] Cf. Rappaport (1998), p. 31.

IT investments will increase or decrease future incomes. But the future incomes do not only depend on the success of IT investments but on numerous other factors such as managerial abilities, behaviour of competitors or overall market situations. Evaluating investments in IT, or companies that have undertaken IT investments, using the ROE may not provide significant information on IT success, due to the fact that the ROE does not especially consider any IT investment characteristics. This statement is fortified by several studies conducted in the 1990s, which did not find any effect of IT investments on ROE.[55] To clarify this, two studies are found useful for a suitability analysis of ROE and ROA for IT investment evaluation and are now shortly illustrated. The two studies, Hitt and Brynjolfsson (1994) and Rai et al. (1997), correspond as far as possible in how the studies were done. Besides some differences, they use comparable data and base on the same methodology of performance measurement. Both studies exceed the analysis of ROE and ROA, but this chapter confines itself to these two performance measures.

Hitt and Brynjolfsson's (1994) analysis at first showed only little, negligible effects of computer capital on ROA.[56] These findings in general confirmed their assumption that computer capital has no effect on ROA and ROE.[57] After expanding their analysis with additional dummy variables for each examined firm, which include firm-specific factors, they found mixed effects of IT on ROA and positive but statistically insignificant effects on ROE.[58]

Rai et al. (1997) found no relationship between IT capital and ROE within their study.[59] They emphasize that ROE not only considers effects of capital investments but also takes financial leverage employed by the firm into account and therefore concluded that "ROE may not be an appropriate criterion for judging the value of IT investments"[60]. In contrast to the findings on ROE a positive relationship between IT capital as well as client/server expenditures and ROA was found.[61]

Considering the results of these studies on ROE and ROA together with the findings on general shortcomings on ROE, ROA

---

[55] Cf. Van der Zee (2002), p. 67.
[56] Cf. Hitt and Brynjolfsson (1994), p. 10.
[57] Cf. Hitt and Brynjolfsson (1994), p. 10.
[58] Cf. Hitt and Brynjolfsson (1994), p. 11.
[59] Cf. Rai David et al. (1997), p. 95.
[60] Rai et al. (1997), p. 95.
[61] Cf. Rai et al. (1997), p. 95.

seems to be more appropriate for judging IT investments than ROE. One factor, previously mention in the suitability analysis of ROI, does also apply to ROE and ROA. They underlie a high degree of arbitrariness. Especially the ROA can be modified by choosing another depreciation policy on the underlying assets.[62] Hence, they both lack of comparability between different firms.

3.2.3   Net present value / Discounted cash flow

3.2.3.1   Theoretical foundation

The basic idea of the net present value (NPV) concept was first introduced by the Yale economist Irving Fisher in 1907.[63] The NPV at time t is obtained by subtracting the costs from the revenues and discounting this difference to the present time. The formula of NPV is as follows:

$$NPV_t = \sum_{t=1}^{T} (R_i - C_i)(1+i)^{(-t)} \quad (t=0,...,T-1)$$

where t represents time, R is revenue impacts, C is cost impacts and i is the discount rate. With the discounting, it pays regard to the time value of money. Whenever the NPV is positive, the project should be carried out. In the case of a negative NPV or if the costs of the asset are greater than the positive NPV value, the project should not be accomplished.

The NPV as well as the DCF approach are based on the assumption that the expected future cash flows are certain. The DCF is computed by discounting the cash flows back to today at a discount rate that reflects the riskiness of those cash flows, which is the main difference to the NPV approach.[64]

$$DCF = \sum_{t=1}^{T} \frac{CF_t}{(1+r)^t} = \frac{CF_1}{(1+r)^1} + \frac{CF_2}{(1+r)^2} + ... + \frac{CF_T}{(1+r)^T}$$

CF_t are the cash flows and r is the risk-adjusted discount rate.

---

[62] Cf. Van der Zee (2002), p. 67.
[63] Cf. Brach (2003), p. 5.
[64] Cf. Brach (2003), p. 4.

"The economic or discounted cash flow (DCF) one-year return for an investment is this year's cash flow plus the change in value over the year, divided by the value at the beginning of the year"[65]:

$$\text{DCF return} = \frac{\text{Cash flow} + \left(\begin{array}{c}\text{Present value at end of year} \\ -\text{Present value at beginning of year}\end{array}\right)}{\text{Present value at beginning of year}}$$

$$= \frac{\text{Cash flow} + \text{Change in present value}}{\text{Present value at beginning of year}}$$

The numerator in the equation above, cash flow + change in present value, represents the economic income.

In contrast to the basic ROI, the DCF takes cash flows over the entire forecast period into account.[66]

3.2.3.2   Suitability analysis

The standard NPV and DCF models are sufficient for valuing most traditional businesses, but it lacks the flexibility to value many new economy companies or others with a similar high share of intangible aspects. It also meets the demands from a share-holder's point of view but is not sufficient for an objective investment evaluation because their computation is dependent on prospects that incorporate subjective expectations. Some researchers on economic and accounting theory judge the NPV to be "the optimum technique to be applied in all situations"[67] while surveys discovered that it is "the least popular of the economic and accounting techniques in practise"[68].

Several objections on the NPV have been found:[69]
- It is an ex-ante figure that relies on estimated future costs and benefits, which are difficult to quantify.

---

[65] Rappaport (1998), p. 21.
[66] Rappaport (1998), p. 23.
[67] King and Mcaulay (1997), p. 131.
[68] King and Mcaulay (1997), p. 131.
[69] For the following three objections confer to King and Mcaulay (1997), p. 131.

- It neglects the aims and perspectives of internal and external stakeholders because the required return rate is not included in the risk-free discount rate.
- The complexity of IT technology is often underestimated and cause-effect relationships are not understood where leading-edge technologies are involved.

Although the NPV and DCF did not prove to be especially suitable for IT investment evaluation because they do not regard many characteristics of these kinds of investments, they are the basis for calculating present values of future returns and other evaluation methods (adjusted ROI, Real options, CFROI and IRR) fall back on this essential concept.

3.2.4   Internal rate of return

3.2.4.1   Theoretical foundation

The internal rate of return (IRR) is defined as the discount rate that results in a net present value of zero for a series of cash flows.

$$NPV(i)_0 = \sum_{i=0}^{T} \frac{CF_i}{(1+i)^i} = 0$$

where i is the internal rate of return and CF are the cash flows.

$$\sum_{i=1}^{T} \frac{CF_i}{(1+i)^i} = \frac{CF_1}{(1+i)^1} + \frac{CF_2}{(1+i)^2} + ... + \frac{CF_T}{(1+i)^T} = 0$$

The IRR is equivalent to the NPV approach with the difference that the equation is solved after i. Under certain circumstances, an investment project can have two internal rates of return, as Figure 1 illustrates (4.6 % and 19.3 %).

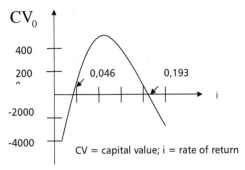

Figure 1: Capital Value Curve; Source: In the style of Franke and Hax (1999), p. 174.

Basically, a project is profitable, if the IRR is greater than the long-term investment rate.

3.2.4.2   Suitability analysis

The IRR bears most of the advantages and disadvantages of the NPV with the exception that it considers the perspectives of internal and external stakeholders because the required return rate, namely the IRR, is included. In the case as described in Figure 3, the investor has to know if the capital values for interest rates between the two internal rates of return are positive or negative, else the knowledge about the two internal rates of return is useless.[70]

Kelleher and MacCormack (2005) highlight that the IRR is based on several dangerous assumptions of which the most dangerous is that interim cash flows, generated by the investment, will be reinvested at the same high rates of return.[71] This can cause problems, if the calculated IRR is higher than the true reinvestment rate for interim cash flows because the measure will then over-estimate the annual equivalent return from the project. They also pointed out that interpreting the IRR as the annual equivalent return on a given investment is only correct, if the project generates no interim cash flows or when the interim cash flows can be invested at the actual IRR. Kelleher and MacCormack (2005) also present results from a study, which found that three-quarters of

---

[70] Cf. Franke and Hax (1999), p. 174.
[71] The following after Kelleher and MacCormack (2005).

CFOs always or almost always use IRR when evaluating capital projects. One reason for this may be that the IRR can be calculated without having to estimate the cost of capital, in contrast to the NPV.[72]

Considering the disadvantages of IRR, Kelleher and MacCormack (2005) came to the conclusion that managers should either stop using the IRR at all or at least use a modified internal rate of return that allows users to set more realistic interim investment rates.[73]

In general, the IRR does not take many of IT investment characteristics into account, equivalent to the NPV and DCF. Considering weaknesses of this measure, found by Kelleher and MacCormack (2005), it is even less suitable for evaluating investments, may they be IT or other kind of investments.

3.2.5   Cash flow return on investment

3.2.5.1   Theoretical foundation

The Cash-Flow-Return on Investment (CFROI) was developed in 1992 by Lewis and Lehmann with the goal to get a metric that should be better at evaluating the operating success or loss of a company than traditional metrics.[74] In contrast to what its name implies, it can only be used to evaluate a whole company or a specific business unit, not a single investment. The CFROI is based upon "the concept of a net present value based on discounted expected cash flows"[75]. The basic idea is that a company is seen as a single investment project with a beginning payout, in the following represented by gross-investment-basis (GIB), and following payment surpluses, represented by gross-cash-flow (GCF) and net value of non-depreciatable assets (NV). CFROI is the rate of interest, which measures the internal return of gross cash flows on gross-investment-basis. The CFROI formula:

$$-\text{GIB} + \sum_{t=1}^{T} \frac{\text{GCF}}{(1+\text{CFROI})^t} + \frac{\text{NV}_T}{(1+\text{CFROI})^T} = 0$$

---

[72] Cf. Value Based Management.net
[73] Cf. Kelleher and MacCormack (2005).
[74] The following after Kloock and Coenen (1996), pp. 1101-1107.
[75] Madden (1999), p. 9.

where t represents time, has to be dissolved towards the CFROI. The necessary computation of GIB, GCF and NV are pointed out as follows:

book value of tangible fixed assets + cumulative depreciations on tangible fixed assets = historic acquisition costs of tangible fixed assets
→ inflating on today's date = updated acquisition value of tangible fixed assets
+ book value of remaining tangible fixed assets + book value of working capital + book value of active accrued and deferred items = updated acquisition costs of assets
- non interest-bearing liabilities = gross-investment-basis (GIB)

Table 4: Computation of the gross-investment-basis; Source: Kloock and Coenen (1996), pp. 1102-1103.

cash-flow of transaction volume - extraordinary income, where affecting payment + extraordinary expenses, where affecting payment + interests and similar expenses + payments-in from disposals of tangible fixed assets (disinvestments) = gross cash flow (GCF)

Table 5: Computation of the gross-cash-flow; Source: Kloock and Coenen (1996), p. 1104.

book value of intangible assets + book value of real estate + book value of financial assets + book value of working capital + book value of active accrued and deferred items - non interest-bearing liabilities = net value of non-depreciatable assets (NV)

Table 6: Computation of net value of non-depreciatable assets; Source: Kloock and Coenen (1996), p. 1104.

At last, the useful life (T in the equation) of tangible fixes assets, that represents the average timeframe for which the tangible fixed assets are at the company's disposal, has to be computed. It is calculated by dividing the historical acquisition costs of tangible fixed assets by the linear depreciation of the respective business period on tangible fixed assets:

$$T = \frac{\text{historical acqisition cos ts of tan gible fixed assets}}{\text{current depreciations}}.$$

A positive CFROI shows that the cash flows generate a positive return on the deployed capital. A negative CFROI indicates that the sum of all cash flows cannot cover the deployed capital.

3.2.5.2   Suitability analysis

A major advantage of the CFROI is its objectivity. Instead of using the annual financial statements, it relies on cash flows and is thereby free of manipulations due to options with regard to items included in the financial statements.[76] Hence it can be used for comparison of different companies unlike most other performance measures. At the same time, the exclusive use of cash flows of the base year is a disadvantage, because investments that are characterized by rising surpluses with advancing lapse of time, such as IT investments whose generation of benefits can last many years, cannot be appraised objectively.[77] Another advantage, especially in the context of IT, is generated by the consideration of all invested capital, including the book value of intangible assets as it can be seen in Table 6.[78] The elimination of several biases is also an advantage of this "total capital concept". It averts the bias caused by different methods of financing as seen by ROI.[79] The use of historic acquisition costs of tangible assets at the end of the business year and not only of the book value of tangible assets also averts the preference of companies with "older" assets and lower book values of these.[80] Companies that follow a "Cash-Out Strategy"[81]

---

[76] Cf. Klook and Coenen (1996), p. 1105.
[77] Cf. Klook and Coenen (1996), p. 1105.
[78] Cf. Klook and Coenen (1996), p. 1105.
[79] Cf. Klook and Coenen (1996), p. 1105.
[80] Cf. Klook and Coenen (1996), p. 1105.

do not show a higher profitability caused by a lower amount of capital.

The setting of a constant cash flow of the base year to the following periods indicates that the CFROI can only mirror the performance of the expired business year, not of future expectations.[82] This problem can partly be solved by a projection of future cash flows, which would reduce the objectivity of this concept. While tangible fixed assets are inflated on today's date as apparent in Table 4, non-depreciatable assets, including intangible assets from IT investments, are set at the book value at the end of the base year as it can be seen in Table 6.[83] Thereby, future rising prices for non-depreciatable assets are not taken into account. Furthermore, payouts for non-capitalizable investments, such as training of personnel or initial advertising are also not considered because the GIB is based upon balance sheet items.[84]

In contrast, Ewert and Wagenhofer (2003) describe one fundamental problem of the CFROI. It may give incentives for underinvestment just as the ROI does. By using cash flows instead of profit, depreciations are unremarkable and by using the internal rate of return, no other interest rates can be included in the calculation.[85]

Generally, the CFROI is a useful metric to show the performance of the operational business from an external view. Concerning IT investments, the CFROI takes intangible costs into account and does not prefer companies that want to increase their performance ratios or stock exchange value by leaving "investments in the future", such as IT investments, undone. Other disadvantages of the CFROI for evaluating IT investments are that it does not include uncertainties, impacts on organizational structures or long-term benefits.

3.2.6   Economic value added

3.2.6.1   Theoretical foundation

---

[81] A Cash-Out strategy indicates that cash flows are not reinvested in the company.
[82] Cf. Klook and Coenen (1996), p. 1106.
[83] Cf. Klook and Coenen (1996), p. 1106.
[84] Cf. Kloock and Coenen (1996), pp. 1106-1107.
[85] Cf. Ewert and Wagenhofer (2003), pp. 558-561.

The economic value added (EVA) was developed and trademarked by the consultant company Stern Steward & Co. with the intension to have a "financial performance measure that comes closer than any other to capturing the true economic profit of an enterprise".[86] It is the difference between net operating profit and a charge for the capital used to deliver that profit:

$$EVA^\circledR = \text{Net operating profit after taxes} \, (\text{NOPAT}) - [\text{Capital} \times \text{The Cost of Capital}]$$

The formula for EVA, provided by Stern Steward & Co., exists in different variants as for the used variable of capital and cost of capital. In German cost accounting for instance, the usually chosen variable for capital is the net operating assets (NOA) and for cost of capital the weighted average cost of capital (WACC).

$$EVA = NOPAT - (NOA \times WACC)$$

As Wagenhofer (2003) noted, EVA is equal to the residual income.[87] It is an entity approach that is total capital-based and the long-term investment rate used to calculate the NOPAT is determined by the WACC that takes the systematic risk of a firm's equity into account in contrast to other financial performance measures.

There are also conversions to be mentioned that can be made to the NOPAT and the invested capital. There are up to 164 conversions suggested in the literature, whose realization would lead to the "True-EVA". Using the "Basic-EVA", as stated above, there are no conversions necessary. Besides the recommendable choice of company specific conversions (Tailored-EVA"), the four most important are:[88]

- *Operating Conversion*: correction of NOPAT and NOA from all non operative components, e.g. non interest-bearing liabilities or extraordinary expenditures and income etc.
- *Funding Conversion*: recordation of all "real" finance, e.g. non-balanced leasing objects and non interest-bearing liabilities etc.
- *Shareholder Conversion*: adaptations for a market-orientated determination of equity and its variances, e.g. activation of expenditures for R&D, advanced training and acquisition of personnel etc.

---

[86] Stern Steward & Co. (2005).
[87] Cf. Ewert and Wagenhofer (2003), p. 536.
[88] For the four main conversions confer Götze and Glaser (2001), pp. 32-33.

- *Tax Conversion*: e.g. tax shield deduction from NOPAT to prevent a double-recordation etc.

Another feature of EVA is the fact that the present value of all future expected EVAs is another metric, namely the market value added (MVA).[89] The MVA reflects the value that the firm has gained beyond the invested capital.

Stern Steward & Co. especially accentuates that the EVA includes the fact that managers have to pay for the capital they employ and therefore showing the monetary affluence a business has created or destroyed per period.[90] They claim that the EVA is a simple and consistent measure that helps managers at their decision making processes by providing them with two principles. First, the primary financial goal is to maximize the wealth of a company's shareholders and secondly, the value of a company depends on the investor's expectations of an excess or shortfall of the profits towards the cost of capital. Hence maximizing the level of EVA maximizes the market value of the firm and so it should meet the demands of all shareholders. "Companies that are experiencing a positive EVA momentum should see their stock market prices go up"[91]. Shareholders will gain a positive value proposition if the return on their equity capital is greater than the costs for equity capital.

Götze and Glaser (2001) agree that EVA and MVA are appropriate measures that help managers to make decisions concerning strategies, projects and other enterprises.[92] They also point out that the inclusion of the firm's equity-risk can be an advantage in comparison to other traditional performance measures that do not take the uncertainties of every investment into account, whereas they reject the use of a period-oriented EVA for the preparation of long-term decisions.

The conversions on EVA have an impact on items of the balance sheet and thus affecting the firm's profit. They add more flexibility to the evaluation of a company by including firm-specific circumstances and therefore mirror the "true value" of a company or project more adequate than others. At the same time a "Tailored EVA" lacks comparability with other firms.

---

[89] Cf. Mengele (1999), pp. 138-139.
[90] Cf. Stern Steward & Co. (2005).
[91] Grants (1997), p. 10.
[92] Cf. Götze and Glaser (2001), pp. 33-34.

No difference to other performance measures is the predict-tion of values in the future, be it profit in the EVA or payments surplus as in the DCF.

3.2.6.2   Suitability analysis

The EVA is a highly sophisticated performance measure that exhibits a high degree of flexibility. Its conversions make an adaptation to firm-specific characteristics possible and in doing so, it can take some characteristics of investments in IT into account. For instance, it considers indirect costs such as training and acqui-sition of personnel and expenditures on intangible assets. How-ever, many characteristics remain unregarded, e.g. intangible and long-term benefits, new business opportunities and uncertainties.

The US Company Alinean developed a measure to "effectively link IT spending with the company's financial performance"[93]. The ROIT™ (Return on IT) is defined as:

$$ROIT = \frac{EVA}{IT\ Spending}$$

where
- EVA = Net profit – Cost of Capital * Shareholder Equity
- Shareholder Equity = Assets – Liabilities
- Cost of Capital is calculated by using the WACC
- IT Spending = Formal IT Spending + Business Unit IT Spending + Indirect (Shadow) IT Spending.[94]

More detailed, IT spending is calculated by ((A * B * Number of Employees) + (C * D * Operating Expenses))* E * F * G, where the coefficients A-F are defined as:
- A = Contribution per Employee TCO to IT spending
- B = Per Employee TCO
- C = Contribution to IT spending as a percentage of Operating Expenses to IT spending
- D = the unit cost IT spending as a percentage of Operating Expenses
- E = the industry factor in IT expenditures
- F = the geographic factor in IT expenditures
- G = company size factor in IT expenditures.[95]

---

[93] Alinean (2005a).
[94] Cf. Alinean (2005a).

These formulas show the distinctive feature of this approach: it is designed to include a company's IT spending, direct and indirect. Alinean claims that "ROIT empowers board members and executives to align IT spending with profitability. It also gives them an invaluable corporate governance tool for measuring and communicating how these IT investments are boosting shareholder value and competitive advantage."[96] A research by Alinean came to the conclusion that the correlation between EVA and IT spending is higher the higher the ROIT rank is.[97] This should fortify the usefulness of ROIT as a profitability measure. But besides the obvious advantages of ROIT towards a "Basic EVA" or other performance measures such as DCF or NPV, which lies mainly in the consideration of all IT costs, it does not take all characteristics of IT investments into account. These are business opportunities, intangible benefits and benefits uncertainty.

3.2.7   Tobin's q

3.2.7.1   Theoretical foundation

Tobin's q is named after its originator James Tobin who invented his q ratio to "measure the incentive to invest in capital"[98]. It associates the (stock) market value of a firm with its replacement costs[99]. If q is greater than one, further investment in capital by the firm will be profitable. If q is less than one, further investment will not be profitable.

$$\text{Tobin's q} = \frac{\text{Market value of a firm}}{\text{Replacement value of total assets}}$$

Tobin's q ratio can basically be used to evaluate whole companies but not single investment projects. The market value of a firm can either be estimated by appropriately adjusting accounting data or in the case of stock market listed corporations, by

---

[95] Cf. Alinean (2005b), p. 6.

[96] Alinean (2005a).

[97] Cf. Johnston (2004).

[98] Abel and Eberly (2003), p. 1.

[99] Replacement costs of an asset are the current costs of purchasing an asset of equivalent productive ability.

their stock market value. The denominator of Tobin's q includes only tangible assets that can be measured and shown in balance sheets, e.g. inventories and property. The numerator of the Tobin's q equation, deduced from the stock market value of a firm, has the advantage that the firm's value now includes intangibles. Some researchers (Brynjolfsson and Yang, 1997; Villalonga, 2004) thereby conclude that subtracting the value of tangible capital stock recorded in the balance sheet from the stock market value would provide the value of a firm's intangible assets.

Tobin's q differs from all other examined measures in one way. It is not an estimated ex ante figure that relies on forecasted cash flows but it relies (ex post) either on existing balance sheet data or on current stock market values.

3.2.7.2   Suitability analysis

Brynjolfsson and Yang (1999) presented evidence that "the estimated average q for computer hardware appears in the order of 10"[100], which is quite high in comparison to the value of 1 for reproducible assets. They identified two sources of this higher q. One source are computer related intangible assets that are composed of capitalized adjustment costs and other intangible assets correlated with computers such as software, new business practises and other complementary organizational innovations.[101] The stream of past adjustment costs is the source for "short term rents", which are earned by the deployed capital and can appear to last longer in the case of computer investments.[102]

According to Brynjolfsson and Yang (1999), the positive effect of investments in computer assets on the stock market value of a firm shall even be higher when they are accompanied by investments in intangible assets. For instance, integration of the computers in the organization, complementary investments and re-engineering of organizational processes are such investments.[103] Another source is that when the accounting principles do not

---

[100] Brynjolfsson and Yang (1999), p. 3.
[101] Cf. Brynjolfsson and Yang (1999), p. 3.
[102] Cf. Brynjolfsson and Yang (1999), p. 4.
[103] Cf. Brynjolfsson and Yang (1999), p. 6.

capture all the firm's productive assets, the denominator of an average q decreases and thereby the overall q increases.[104]

Brynjolfsson and Yang (1999) found in their study that "each dollar in computer capital is associated with over $16 of market value...this implies, that the stock market imputes an average of $15 of "intangible assets" to a firm for every $1 of computer capital"[105].

However, from the point of view in the year 2006, their results do not appear too impressive anymore because this study was done shortly before the burst of the so called "Internet Bubble"[106], which confirms the suspicion that this valuation may be overrated. One should also be aware of the fact that stock markets are not efficient in any case and market valuations include other values such as expectations on future cash flows, growth opportunities or overall economic development.

In general, Tobin's q is especially popular in evaluating firms that undertake R&D investments because it takes intangible assets and benefits that arise form these investments into account. Hence, it is just as useful to evaluate companies that invest in information technology, whose intangible aspects are remarkable. Although stock market valuations are not fully mathematical verifiable, they include some IT investments characteristics like no other financial performance measure. Analysts and rating agencies can consider aspects in their valuation that are not quantifiable but contribute to a firm's positive or negative development. In the case of IT investments, these can be benefits and costs that arise from intangible assets, complementary investments, organizational changes, new business opportunities and uncertainties.

For people who trust in stock market valuations, Tobin's q can thereby be the one business ratio that pays regard to IT investment characteristics like no other. To get a value for a single IT investment of a firm, one has to compare the q value before and after the investment. Hence it is useful at an ex-post view. Using Tobin's q for an ex-ante consideration, one could compare observed changes in the q value after past IT investments and estimate if these effects could apply to the considered future

---

[104] Cf. Brynjolfsson and Yang (1999), p. 4.

[105] Brynjolfsson and Yang (1999), p. 18.

[106] Around 2000 the stock market value of most listed "internet companies", whose assets were mainly intangible, had fallen dramatically when people suddenly assumed their stock market value to be strongly overrated.

investment, which is difficult due to their complexity. An announcement of an IT investment, when it has a strategic value, can cause a direct positive reaction on the stock market.[107] Thereby the expected effects of this investment are revealed, which is still not useful when the decision for the investment has to be made before the announcement. Hence, an ex-ante evaluation is necessary.

3.2.8   Real options

3.2.8.1   Theoretical foundation

Some of the previous mentioned evaluation measures can be historically traced back to the beginning of the 20th century, but real options are no invention of the 20th century. Some researchers traced the use of options on real assets back to the year 1728 or even earlier.[108] This shows that the basic concept of acquiring options on future assets is a rather simple and intuitive concept. However, the first mathematical formula on options, the so called Black-Scholes formula, which assumes that the costs of a project are known with certainty and has been developed for financial options in the first place, was introduced in 1973. M. Scholes and R. Merton, together with the late F. Black, later received the Nobel Prize for their work on this concept.[109] This formula paved the way for the concept of "real options" developed by Stewart Meyers in 1977.[110] Meyers later advanced this concept to the real options analysis, followed by many other researchers on that field.

In contrast to some conventional approaches, the real options model takes the risks and opportunities created by deferring, expanding, contracting, abandoning, switching use or altering investments in the future into consideration.[111] The fundamental difference towards traditional measurement methods as DCF or NPV, where the expected future cash flows are assumed certain, is that the real options approach considers the future as

---

[107] Dehning and Richardson (2002), p. 21.
[108] Cf. Brach (2003), pp. 13-14.
[109] Cf. Baecker and Hommel (2003), p. 2.
[110] Cf. Brach (2003), pp. 14-15.
[111] Cf. Lei and Rawles (2003), p. 80.

unpredictable.[112] Hence, it can provide us with a framework which can assist decision makers at their decision making process under uncertainty. Uncertainty in a project's payoffs and the time lag between investment and its recoupments are considered to have positive influences on the value of an investment opportunity.[113] The essence of the real options approach can best be expressed with the words:

"flexibility creates value"[114].

Broyles (2003) illustrated a simple numerical example that clarifies this statement.[115] The initial point is a company that could invest in a new product in two years by engaging in research and development now. They assume that the NPV of the project will be €10 million with a probability of 50 percent and minus €10 million with the same probability. The expected NPV would be:

$$0.5 \times 10m + 0.5 \times (-10m) = 0.$$

Including now that managers have the option but not the obligation to invest in a project that leads to a negative NPV, the calculation is as follows:

$$0.5 \times 10m + 0.5 \times 0 = 5 \, \text{million}.$$

This shows that being able to make a choice is valuable. In this case, the choice, or real option, has a value of €5 million. The additional value created by the option in comparison to the NPV is also called option premium. The executives in this example should continue to invest in R&D as long as the expenditure is less than the €5 million. Broyles (2003) in addition showed that a real options value increases the more uncertainty, hence more risk is involved. To proof this statement, the example's assumptions are varied in the way that the project now leads either to a NPV of €20 million or to minus €20 million:

$$0.5 \times 20m + 0.5 \times 0 = 10m$$

A doubling of the involved risk has doubled the value of the option, because managers do not have to invest on the downside. They could now invest up to 10 million in R&D.

Critics of the real options approach could reply to these findings that it only applies to cases in which it is possible to

---

[112] Cf. Howell et al. (2001), p. 2.

[113] Cf. Kumaraswamy (1996), p. 12.

[114] Baecker and Hommel (2003), p. 2.

[115] The following example after Broyles (2003), p. 38.

control the downside risk by stopping projects immediately. Therefore, executives would have to be informed about a possible future failure of the project, which in practise is quite difficult.

The real options approach is principally based on calculating a NPV. Another possibility would be to do it in terms of market, income or cost approach, namely the DCF or similar approaches.[116] To calculate such a NPV, future revenues have to be predicted. Different methods can be used to achieve that, e.g. time-series forecasting, simulation, regression, cross sectional or stochastic models, depending on the circumstances and availability of historical data.[117] A widely used approach in that field is the so called "Monte Carlo Simulation" which also considers the volatility of a project. A Monte Carlo simulation is a kind of spreadsheet simulation, which randomly generates values for uncertain variables over and over, allowing one to see the probabilities of different possible outcomes of an investment strategy.[118]

The real options analysis tries to answer the questions at what cost one should sell or buy an option and when one should exercise an option.[119]

Before trying to understand the whole concept, we should begin with defining what an option actually is. "An option gives you the right, in an uncertain future, to pick whatever action will turn out to be "the best of" two or more actions, as the uncertain future unfolds"[120]. Most of the possible forms of options used in practise are:

- *Call option* - the right to acquire an asset at a previously defined future date for a now known cost, no matter how much the market value of the asset may change meanwhile.[121]
- *Put option* – "the right to sell an asset in future, at a price known now, whatever its market selling price may be at that time"[122].
- *Barrier option* – a combination of put and call options. When the asset value breaches an artificial barrier, the option becomes in-the-money or out-of-the-money.[123]

---

[116] Cf. Mun (2003), p. 41.
[117] Cf. Mun (2003), p. 41.
[118] Cf. Mun (2003), p. 61.
[119] Cf. Howell et al. (2001), p. 13.
[120] Howell et al. (2001), p. 13.
[121] Cf. Howell et al. (2001), p. 4.
[122] Howell et al. (2001), p. 4.

- *European option* – "option which gives the right to invest (or to sell out) on only one fixed future date"[124].
- *American option* - option that gives the right to invest or sell out at a point in time of someone's own choice, which is usually defined in advance.[125]
- *Perpetual option* – "option which will never expire"[126].
- *Exchange option* –two or more values vary randomly and one has the right to choose one of them in the future.[127]
- *Compound option* – "the value of the option depends on the value of another option"[128].

The underlying asset of an option can be undeveloped real estate and oil fields, factory capacities and equipment, or long-term investment opportunities such as R&D or IT investment projects that yield uncertain payoffs.[129]

3.2.8.2   Suitability analysis

As the theoretical background for real options analysis is given, it will be useful to see the effects of real options in practise. Therefore, the use of the real options analysis on IT will be exemplified by a consolidation of data marts into an enterprise data warehouse (EDW). This study, done by Jeffery et al. (2003), will be summarized in the following:[130]

"A data mart is a database that is most often associated with a specific business unit, business process, or customer segment"[131]. Thus, it is separated from other databases. Jeffery et al. (2003) identified the following tangible benefits of consolidating these databases into a companywide data warehouse:
- It enables its users to get all information necessary to create a single view of and a single voice to the customer.[132]

---

[123] Cf. Mun (2003), p. 171.
[124] Howell et al. (2001), p. 4.
[125] Cf. Howell et al. (2001), p. 4.
[126] Howell et al. (2001), p. 4.
[127] Cf. Howell et al. (2001), p. 4.
[128] Mun (2003), p. 136.
[129] Cf. Kumaraswamy (1996), p. 11.
[130] The following case study after Jeffery et al. (2003).
[131] Jeffery et al. (2003), p. 8.
[132] Cf. Jeffery et al. (2003), pp. 8-9.

- Reduced total cost of ownership because often different vendors support multiple data marts, which can now be changed into one single vendor supporting the data ware-house (better service contract; fewer personnel; reduced overhead; personnel has to be trained on only one system).[133]
- Reduced data and system redundancies and higher quality of data.[134]
- "CRM analytic applications can be more efficiently run on a fully consolidated EDW"[135].

During the study, several characteristics of this project became apparent. The most important are uncertainty and risk respectively towards the adherence of its time schedule and bud-get as well as the realization of its expected benefits, due to its complexity and the need for organizational changes.[136] Other uncertainties that have an effect on the success of the project are: "scalability of the solution, reliance on external IT help, changes in job skills and personnel displacement, training, organizational poli-tics, cultural issues, lack of insight and vision, and lack of focus on overall objectives of data warehousing efforts"[137].

Jeffery et al. (2003) divided the 15 data marts into smaller phases. This approach has the advantage that it increases flexibility. Executives then have the option to abandon or continue the project after the results of the implementation of the previous phase are clear. Therefore, it was divided into five or ten data marts within each phase. For deciding on how many phases are "best", three scenarios were calculated.

1. A consolidation of all 15 data marts in one single phase, which offers no option and can thereby be calculated using the DCF approach.
2. Two phases with a pilot-phase of 5 data marts and 10 following in the second phase.
3. Three phases with 5 data marts in each phase.

All the cash flows and costs of the base case as well as their changes in the proposed consolidation are basically assumptions. In this example Jeffery et al. (2003) saddled themselves with interviewing EDW implementation consultants and other experts

---

[133] Cf. Jeffery et al. (2003), p. 9.
[134] Cf. Jeffery et al. (2003), p. 13.
[135] Cf. Jeffery et al. (2003), p. 13.
[136] Cf. Jeffery et al. (2003), p. 9.
[137] Jeffery et al. (2003), p. 10.

to gain the best information possible on the volatility and uncertainty parameters respectively in this project. They gathered information about the expected, maximum, minimum values and their standard deviations, which are then used in Monte Carlo simulations to determine the overall volatility of the project return. The volatility of the project phases is based upon 10.000 Monte Carlo simulation runs of the underlying cash flows.[138] The most important of these parameters are the implementation project schedule and personnel staff reductions "that are directly obser- vable and that will have a high impact on the actual returns and their volatility"[139]. Although there are more factors, only these two were included in the analysis.

The real options of scenarios 2 and 3 are calculated using the binomial approach. A general example for such a binominal tree is illustrated in Figure 2. From the options tree, one can also derive that the options in this example are "european", because the options can only be done at a specific date, and "compound" options because if an option can be taken or not depends on the choice of previous options.

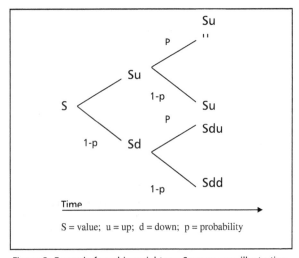

Figure 2: Example for a binomial tree; Source: own illustration.

---

[138] Cf. Jeffery et al. (2003), p. 7.
[139] Jeffery et al. (2003), pp. 23-24.

The results of these calculations are summarized as follows. The NPV of the base case is 3.139.259$. In case of scenario 2 (two-stage project) using a 1-step binomial real options approach the NPV is 6.800.909$ and the option premium 696.779$, which is generated by the flexibility provided by the option.[140] The NPV for scenario three (three-stage project) is 4.758.619$ and the option value 909.635$. The option premium of the three-phase strategy is bigger than that of the two-phase strategy. This shows that the additional option available at the three-phase strategy creates additional value.

When analyzing the suitability of the real options approach for evaluating IT investments, one has to be aware of the assumptions that are made to the Black-Scholes approach. Jeffery et al. (2003) found that the Black-Scholes formula relies on a number of assumptions that limit their applicability to valuing real options. These assumptions are:[141]

- "There is only one real option modelled and valued at a time. So, the option is contingent on only one underlying asset. This assumption restricts the applicability of the Black-Scholes model to value compound options, which consist of more that one real option".
- "There is only one source of uncertainty (that is, only one uncertainty can be dealt at one time) and the variance is known and constant".
- "The risk free rate is constant and known".
- "The underlying asset does not pay any dividends".
- "The options are European (can expire only at maturity)".
- "The exercise price is known and constant (that is, expected cost to implement the project cannot change)".
- "Market are complete, the firm is risk-neutral, or risk is fully diversifiable".

These assumptions limit the Black-Scholes approach to certain kinds of options and reduce its touch for reality. Because the first assumption does not apply to the examined project, the binomial model must be used for this three-phase compound option valuation.[142]

In general, the real options approach provides a powerful framework for thinking about corporate value. The example of

---

[140] Cf. Jeffery et al. (2003), p. 28.
[141] The following assumptions are cited after Jeffery et al. (2003), pp. 22-23.
[142] Cf. Jeffery et al. (2003), p. 23.

Jeffery et al. (2003) has brilliantly shown how flexibility creates value. From all examined evaluation methods, only the real options approach pays regard to this flexibility and uncertainty. But also this concept bears several shortcomings. The use of the Black-Scholes formula, which was primarily developed for financial markets, for valuing real options has several weaknesses. It is based on several assumptions that do not apply to real options, e.g. the returns must be log-normally distributed, securities must be continuously traded, there must be complete markets that provide an unlimited number of options to trade with, units and fractions of units on securities can be traded, and volatility does not change overtime.[143] However, the many kinds of real options analysis that have been developed over time have eliminated most of these Black-Scholes shortcomings. E.g. the binomial option pricing model can work with changing volatility.[144]

In practise, a gap between the calculated value of companies' investment projects using real options approaches and the later realized value is noticeable. It may be the result of a disconnection between the way managers value options and the way they manage them.[145]

As the real options approach uses NPV calculations, it bears the same shortcomings. Direct and measurable indirect costs and benefits can be considered, but business opportunities, long-term benefits and organizational changes are not taken into account.

3.2.9   Total cost of ownership

3.2.9.1   Theoretical foundation

The main conclusion of the total cost of ownership (TCO) study, conducted by the Gartner Group in 1996 that introduced this concept for the first time, was that the TCO of a well managed computer environment are roughly 25 to 40 percent lower than that of a typical PC/LAN environment.[146] TCO "is the total cost of a computer asset throughout its life cycle..., from acquisition to

---

[143] Cf. Brach (2003), p. 331.
[144] Cf. Brach (2003), p. 332.
[145] Cf. Copeland and Tufano (2004), p. 91.
[146] Cf. Groh (1997), p. 42.

disposal"[147]. It is often used to measure the effectiveness of a company's IT expenditures and can possibly help to reduce the overall costs associated with ownership of computer assets.[148] Table 7 gives an overview of TCO cost factors.

The Gartner Group study figured out that of these cost factors acquisition costs take up to 20 percent of the TCO.[149] Futz factors make up about one third of end-user costs, training 18 percent of overall costs, manipulation of system resources about 15 percent, end-user scripting about 14 percent and informal learning activities circa 13 percent.[150] Another important conclusion from the study is that non-budgeted costs, such as hidden end-user costs, are doubling all operating costs over the following five years.[151] Managers who aim at maximizing the value of IT expenditures have to reduce the TCO.[152] TCO reduction by reducing the acquisition costs is quite difficult because computer hard- and software have become commodities and a possible discount at their acquisition will not contribute to an advantage towards competitors who will most likely get the same discount. The highest potential for savings lies at the 80 percent share of the TCO, the administration costs. Control costs are an optional investment but can contribute to a reduction of operations costs. Both options, centralization and standardization, may lead to reduced operations costs.

---

[147] Lei and Rawles (2003), p. 79.
[148] Cf. Smith David et al. (2003), pp. 101-102.
[149] Cf. Groh (1997), p. 42.
[150] Cf. Groh (1997), p. 42.
[151] Cf. Groh (1997), p. 42.
[152] The following after Smith David et al. (2003), pp. 102-104.

Cost Category	Cost Factors	Examples
Acquisition costs	Hardware	Monitors, CPUs, servers.
	Software	Operating systems, database management systems, word processors.
Control costs	Centralization	Specialized hardware (such as intelligent self-monitoring components that notify a network management console when a problem occurs) and software (such as directory services and desktop management interfaces) are needed to implement and maintain a centralized system. Support staff has to be trained to use these systems.
	Standardization	Non-standard hardware and software may have to be replaced by hardware and software conforming to the selected standards. Users may have to be retrained in the standard software and the standard hardware may be more expensive than the non-standard hardware.
Operations costs	Support	Either in-house staff or support contract is required to address hardware and software problems as they arise.
	Evaluation	Question such as "Does it do what it is supposed to do? And is it compatible to the existing IT environment?" have to be cleared before upgrading or replacing applications.
	Installation / Upgrade	The installation and upgrading of new technology, consisting of hardware and software, has to be done after the evaluation.
	Training	Either formal training in a classroom setting or self-training as end users learn how to work new applications.
	Downtime	Downtime arises when hardware and software failures, installations and upgrades occur. The costs consist of nonworking systems and employees and of repair time and personnel.
	Futz	Bill Kirwin of Gartner Group defines the "futz factors" as "using corporate technology for your own personal use."
	Auditing	Costs of keeping track of an organization's technology assets, mostly done by some sort of report keeping.
	Virus	Viruses can destroy important data that has to be recreated or can cause computers to crash, resulting in downtime.
	Power consumption	Published estimates put electric power consumption at $250 per year per workstation. Computers can also generate heat, which can increase air-conditioning costs.

Table 7: TCO cost factors; Source: Smith David et al. (2003), pp. 102-103.

To emphasize this statement, a few advantages of the two follow. Some of the many advantages of centralized control are:[153]
- Support costs are reduced because troubleshooting can be done from a central location.

---

[153] The following advantages after Smith David et al. (2003), p. 104.

- Upgrading costs are reduced when software is centrally located on only a few servers.
- Downtime and the number of support people are reduced when end users have no control over applications and thus cannot damage or change it.
  Some advantages of standardization are:
- Less personnel training is necessary.
- Less diversity in computer hard- and software reduces auditing costs.
- Anti-virus software is easier and on more workstation installed and thus reduces support and downtime costs.

Smith David et al. (2003) also examined the connection between reducing TCO and the quality of IT service levels. Although the connection seems to be directly proportional, the analysis concluded that there is a way to reduce TCO without reducing service levels or even to improve them. In order to achieve this, the existing IT infrastructure has to be examined towards its readiness for a centralized control, a comprehensive implementation plan has to be developed and user buy-in has to be ensured, which would increases the likelihood of its acceptance. The last point can be achieved if special communication channels are established, end users are involved in the planning process and user feedback is collected through surveys and face-to-face meetings.

Riverbank et al. (2001) recommends the following procedure of computing a TCO:

- Mapping the process and determining the TCO categories,
- determining the cost elements for each category and deciding how each cost element is measured, and
- involving the gathering of data and the quantification of costs,

while a cost timeline should also be constructed for the length of the life cycle and the present value of all costs should be calculated.[154]

3.2.9.2   Suitability analysis

Smith David et al. (2003) recommend a benefit/cost analysis to be done before deciding for more control to reduce the TCO.[155]

---

[154] Cf. Riverbank et al. (2001), p. 55.

It has to be cleared in advance that all costs associated with implementing the control mechanism and the possible degradations in service levels do not exceed the long-term cost savings in operations.[156]

Several problems occur when calculating the TCO of a project. Different companies or analysts define TCO terms differently, possibly due to a focus on marketing.[157] Indirect costs are difficult to measure and even the calculation of direct costs can be problematic because of insufficient inventory and misleading budget data.[158] Groh (1997) concluded that the TCO calculation is not globally valid and a definition of goals in advance is absolutely necessary.[159] According to Gartenberg (2000) a TCO study can help making senior management aware of the complexities of distributed computing, justify budget and staffing requirements and even warns that without an understanding of TCO, IT organizations may face eventual disaster and extinction.[160]

However, the main goal of the TCO is to gain knowledge and control over all costs that are associated with computer assets and possibly reduce them. And this is already the only aspect of IT investments that is considered in this concept. It neglects intangible benefits, impact on organizational structure and uncertainties completely. Therefore, TCO is not an appropriate concept to measure the profitability of IT investments.

3.3 Result overview

Table 8 illustrates for each previously analyzed evaluation measure, if and to what extent the IT investment characteristics are taken into account.

---

[155] Smith David et al. (2003), pp. 105.
[156] Smith David et al. (2003), pp. 105.
[157] Cf. Groh (1997), p. 44.
[158] Cf. Groh (1997), p. 44.
[159] Cf. Groh (1997), p. 44.
[160] Cf. Gartenberg (2000)

Characteristics / Measures	Direct Costs	Indirect Costs	Intangible Assets	Long-term Benefits	New Business Opportunities	Organizational Changes	Cost Uncertainty	Benefits Uncertainty
Amortization / Payback	++	-	-	-	-	-	-	-
Basic ROI	++	+	+	-	-	-	-	-
Adjusted ROI	++	++	++	-	-	+	-	-
ROE	++	+	+	-	-	-	-	-
ROA	++	+	+	-	-	-	-	-
NPV / DCF	++	+	-	-	-	-	-	-
IRR	++	+	-	-	-	-	-	-
CFROI	++	+	+	-	-	-	-	-
EVA	++	+	+	-	-	-	-	-
ROIT	++	++	+	-	-	-	-	-
Tobin's q	++	+	+	+	+	+	+	+
Real options	++	+	-	-	-	-	++	++
TCO	++	++	-	-	-	-	-	-

Table 8: Correlation between IT investment characteristics and financial evaluation measures; Source: own illustration.

Legend: -   → factor is **not** taken into account or has **negative influence** on the measure

+   → factor is **partly** taken into account

++ → factor is **fully** taken into account

Attention, in the appraisal of the suitability of the examined measures, should be paid to the fact that all these measures are used in management accounting and not for financial reporting. Hence, they underlie a certain degree of arbitrariness because basically they are not controlled and can be modified as desired. Still, in the following appraisal the author of this work acts on the assumption that the measures are not intentionally manipulated and are calculated according to their theoretical foundations.

Amortization / Payback: The only characteristic that is taken fully into account is direct costs, such as initial investment costs. All others are neglected.

Basic ROI: Of all characteristics only the costs and intangible assets are taken into account and of these only the direct costs completely. Indirect costs are only partly regarded because e.g. downtime cannot be included in the book value of assets in the ROI equation. Intangible assets can partly be included, but this depends on the respective accounting standard. German HGB, US-GAAP and IAS consider an activation of certain but not all intangible assets at different values.

Adjusted ROI: In contrast to the basic ROI, the adjusted ROI is more flexible and can include indirect costs and intangible assets as desired and as far as they can be measured and a value can be assigned to them. Organizational changes, in the form of a change in process costs, are also included.

ROE / ROA: ROE and ROA basically share the same results as the basic ROI. However, the ROA was found to be the more appropriate measure for evaluating IT investments because there was no correlation between IT capital and ROE found in the examined studies.

NPV / DCF / IRR: The NPV, DCF and IRR only consider costs as long as they are measurable, while all other characteristics are neglected.

CFROI: Direct costs are completely regarded, whereas indirect costs and intangible assets are only partially considered in the CFROI.

EVA / ROIT: The EVA is also very flexible due to its conversions, and can consider most costs and many intangible assets. The ROIT even pays more regard to cost factors and includes all tangible and intangible costs that are measurable and quantifiable.

Tobin's q: Tobin's q is the only measure that takes all aspects of IT investments, at least partly, into account. Partly, because the market value of a firm may be over or understated and is therefore not fully objective.

Real options: Measurable direct and indirect costs are considered, but the outstanding attribute of the real options approach is its consideration of uncertainties towards the success and failure of investment projects.

TCO: The TCO is limited on the cost side of an investment, which is undeniably well done.

Counting the number of + marks, the "losers" in the contest for the best evaluation measure for IT investments are amortization / payback, NPV, DCF, IRR and TCO. This result supports the opinion that a project appraisal alone relying on one of these evaluation measures is not advisable. They should always be accompanied by other ratios that contribute more insight to an appraisal. However, many evaluation measures, such as real options analysis and adjusted ROI, cannot work without including NPV calculations. Hence, the NPV is a must for project evaluation. The amortization method can be a useful measure for evaluating projects of low complexity and fast recoupment and can provide managers with information about a project's efficiency but its many disadvantages advises one not to rely on it alone. The single use of IRR is not advisable or at least it should be replaced by a modified IRR. Using the TCO, one has to be aware of the fact hat it is limited to calculating costs.

Tobin's q is the "winner" in this contest, followed by real options and adjusted ROI. The success of Tobin's q may be that it depends on the basic principle of a free market economy: the interplay of supply and demand, included in the equation by the market value of a firm. As the only examined evaluation measure it takes all IT investment characteristics, at least partly, into account. Furthermore, its strong points are the consideration of intangible aspects, such as new business opportunities enabled by previous IT investments and their possible long-term benefits, which are not considered by any other examined evaluation measure. The real options analysis combines the basic NPV approach and possible risks and choices in investment decisions. The adjusted ROI also combines different basic approaches, namely the basic ROI, NPV and valuation of intangible assets.

Evidently, the "losers" are simple limited approaches that are best used when investment outcomes and costs are certain and quantitative. This is backed by King and Mcaulay (1997) who stated that "ROI measures are the most suitable where the outcomes are certain, the system is the support rather than core and quantitative rather than qualitative benefits are typical of the environment within which the evaluation is undertaken"[161]. The winning evaluation measures combine different approaches enabling them to take quantitative and qualitative aspects into account.

---

[161] King and Mcaulay (1997), p. 132.

It is imperative to emphasize that financial evaluation measures cannot measure IT effectiveness. Examples for IT effectiveness are support of business processes, activities and employees.[162] The TCO is an exception to that rule, because it can measure how effectively IT spending is deployed.

---

[162] Cf. Van der Zee (2002), p. 4.

4   IT investment evaluation in practise

4.1 Status quo

If a vendor wants to sell his products to the customer, he has to make sure that the customer can understand his arguments supporting the product. Hence, the ROI is the most commonly used evaluation measure concerning IT investments. Its simplicity and understandability has paved the way for its worldwide proliferation. Every businessman and people without any connection to the business world will easily understand that a return on investment of any positive percentage figure is a good thing. Although there might be more suitable evaluation measures for certain situations, the reluctance to actually use them in considerations is a phenomenon seen in practise.

Despite the many advantages of the real options approach, Baecker and Hommel (2003) observed an increasing detachment of it from real-world applications. Signs for this development are that consulting firms do not bring real options forward as a core competence. If they do, they do not use real options terminology while communicating with clients or investment bankers, and venture capitalists do not apply the real options method likewise.[163]

The return on management (ROM), developed by Strassmann during the 1990s, is a good example for the matter of fact that even measures of financial performance through IT which are assumed to be theoretically valid, do not always become largely accepted.[164]

Some vendors developed their own methods to show the payback of the products they offer. The industry researcher Giga Information Group for example uses a methodology called Total Economic Impact™ (TEI) to measure a project's viability.[165] Alinean uses the ROIT to link IT spending to a firm's financial performance. If one of these developed methods will become widely accepted or not is unclear. The TCO, developed by the Gartner Group in 1996, is an example for such a method that has become an accepted standard in practise.

---

[163] Cf. Baecker and Hommel (2003), p. 32.
[164] Cf. Van der Zee (2002), pp. 66-67.
[165] Cf. Plesman Publications and Gale Group (2002).

Many software providers use so called "ROI-Calculators", which are a popular shortening of financial success calculation and are based on information provided by potential customers or employers or benchmarking studies.[166] The given data are rough estimates, thus these calculations can only give a first indication for the possible success of such investment projects. Others judge such calculators as useful tools that include all financial formulae and intangible aspects and emphasize its usefulness when applied to all projects in a company. A reduction in time needed to prepare a ROI calculation is also one of its advantages.[167]

A phenomenon that can be seen in practise is that only a minority of companies that invest in new IT define their financial goals in advance. Most people seem to simply trust in the useful-ness of these systems and rely on "soft" targets such as better customer satisfaction. This assumption is backed by an internet executive e-panel survey about ROI conducted by the International Data Corporation in 2000. It has been discovered that two-thirds of the asked executives do not use ROI for an e-business project calculation.[168] Reasons for this may be that the effort necessary for calculating an imperfect ROI is assumed to be too high, that there is not enough data to base calculations on, because the ROI of e-business applications is usually positive and when similar companies have already been calculating a ROI.[169]

Past surveys, including interviews with executives on the use of evaluation measures, found out that financial directors often do not rely on only one single method but use several in combination, such as NPV, IRR and Payback, although one can get contrary results.[170] Thereby, the executives prevent that an inappropriate or solely use of a single standard financial performance measure, such as NPV, DCF and others, would result in the mistaken rejection of worthwhile long-term investment opportunities, thereby biasing the firm's investment decisions toward short-term profits.[171] These executives also pointed out that due to "expec-tations out there" and the influence of the financial markets, the

---

[166] Cf. Lee (2001), p. 11.
[167] Cf. Mogollon and Raisinghani (2004), p. 211.
[168] Cf. Mogollon and Raisinghani (2004), p. 188.
[169] Cf. Mogollon and Raisinghani (2004), p. 188.
[170] Cf. King and Mcaulay (1997), p. 136.
[171] Cf. Kumaraswamy (1996), p. 2.

absolute impact on profit has to be considered.[172] The satisfaction of stakeholders in general plays an important role in firm strategies as well as the corporate image seen by externals that can affect decisions of executives.

Therefore, it is necessary to take a view on the motivation of decision makers to make certain decisions. To assume that they behave and decide as a "homo oeconomicus"[173] is simply unrealistic. Individuals are subjects to preferences and dislikes that influence their decisions. Managers, whose salaries depend on the stock price of companies, may decide for strategies that boost the stock price for the short-term and thereby act against long-term goals. This is generally characterized under the term "principal-agency problem", which describes the issue that managers (agents) do not always act in the best interest of the shareholders (principals).

4.2 Evaluation and suggestions for improvements on status quo

Besides the description of many evaluation techniques and their advantages and disadvantages in chapter 3, it is the author's opinion that it is impossible to name one single method that is the best to evaluate investments in IT in all cases. Farbey et al. (1994) also pointed out that the complexity of IT investments and their many characteristics lead to a wide range of circumstances in which these investments have to be applied.[174] The same complexity of characteristics and circumstances applies to the different evaluation methods. Therefore, finding an appropriate framework that matches these two factors is the goal to be achieved.

There are various frameworks and categorizations to be found in the research literature on that field. Farbey et al. (1994) for example focus on a 2 x 2 matrix, which matches a conservative and a radical role of IT to well defined and fuzzy evaluation constraints. For well defined evaluation constraints and conser-

---

[172] Cf. King and Mcaulay (1997), p. 136.

[173] The lightly humorous term „homo oeconomicus" describes a person who acts and decides economical and under complete rationality.

[174] Farbey et al. (1994), p. 239.

vative IT, the ROI is advised.[175] When the role of IT is radical a cost benefit analysis shall be used. Fuzzy evaluation constraints and a conservative role of IT should require experimental methods and others. To a radical role of IT information economics, return on management, boundary values and critical success factors are assigned.

Riverbank et al. (2001) recommends a three-tiered set of business case methodologies, which are scaled to the size and complexity of a project.[176] Tier 1 represents least complex and least cost intensive projects. The recommended metric for such projects is the TCO. Tier 2 (middle/cost) initiatives should be measured by TCO, payback period, benefit/cost ratio, internal rate of return or return on investment. For tier 3 (most complex/cost), applied information economics are advised.

In the following (see Table 9), the author of this book suggests a framework, which assigns IT investment evaluation measures to an appropriate IT investment category. The used category is the degree of tangibility. A high degree of tangibility encloses IT with solely tangible characteristics. These tangible characteristics include all quantifiable aspects that can be expressed monetarily, such as costs for acquisition, ongoing costs, cost reductions and measurable returns in the form of cash flows. A middle degree of tangibility encloses IT with tangible aspects and in addition intangible assets that can be expressed in monetary values, e.g. self-developed software. A low degree of tangibility encloses IT that applies to the previous category and furthermore exhibits intangible characteristics, which include nonmonetary aspects, such as intangible assets that cannot be valued monetarily, benefits from organizational changes, long-term benefits, uncertainties and new business opportunities

---

[175] Cf. Farbey et al. (1994), p. 239.

[176] Cf. Riverbank et al. (2001), p. 23.

IT Investments' Tangibility		
High	Middle	Low
Amortization / Payback NPV / DCF / IRR TCO	Basic ROI ROA EVA CFROI	(Adjusted ROI) Tobin's q Real options

Table 9: Financial evaluation measures for IT investments; Source: own illustration.

The found attribution of financial evaluation measures to IT investment categories does pay regard to a necessary abidance of commensurability. Evaluation measures, which combine different concepts and are more complex and sophisticated, such as Tobin's q and real options, are assigned for evaluating IT investments of high intangibility and complexity, which contribute a lot to a company. The effort needed to conduct such an evaluation is justifiable. Projects of low complexity, high tangibility and low contribution to the firm value demand for evaluation methods, whose efforts do not exceed their values. An amortization or ROI calculation may be the better choice in the case of investing in a new piece of hardware, while a companywide implementation of an ERP or CRM system demands for more detailed analysis. The adjusted ROI, assigned to IT investments of low tangibility in Table 9 and set in brackets, is not the most suitable measure for evaluation in this category because it takes only two of the intangible aspects of that category into account, but it is neither limited to these kind of investments. It can also be applied to the other two categories, due to the fact that everyone is familiar with the way of its calculation and available ROI calculators even reduce the effort needed for the calculation. The reverse conclusion that evaluation measures assigned to investments of high tangibility can be applied to the other two categories cannot be made. A Tobin's q and real options calculation for investments of high tangibility is also not advisable. Tobin's q was found to be useful at quantifying the value of intangible assets, organizational changes, long-term benefits and uncertainties caused by IT investments. One of its strong points is that it can be used to gain the value of intangible assets. The equation would then be:

Intangible assets = value of a firm's financial securities – tangible capital stock[177].
However, the gained figure from this equation would still only be an estimation.

The suggested approach of Table 9, aligned with IT invest-ment characteristics, shows similarities to the approach of Riverbank et al. (2001). From tier 1 to tier 3 the complexity of the technology and the evaluation technique increases and from investments of high tangibility to low tangibility their complexity and the complexity of the assigned evaluation measure increases too. Even the approach of Farbey et al. (1994) bears resemblance in the way that they differentiate between a conservative role of IT, which indicates that this kind of technology is standardized and hence well known from previous projects and uncomplicated in the implementation process, and a radical role of IT, which indi-cates an innovative more complex technology. Although all these approaches differ in the examined evaluation techniques and to a minor degree in the found classification of IT, they all have the association of a certain complexity of evaluation methods to the same complexity of the technologies in common.

A different approach in order to better evaluate investments is best described by the words of Steve Flammini, CTO at Partners Healthcare in Boston: "We define success before we pilot the technology, then test afterward"[178]. Defining success and object-ives that have to be reached in advance, not only enables a target-oriented proceeding of the implementation process, but also makes it easier to measure the success or failure of a project because it is possible to orientate oneself on a standard of comparison.

---

[177] Derived from Brynjolfsson and Yang (1999), p. 5.
[178] Dix (2004).

5   Conclusions and outlook

This book tries to answer several questions concerning the suitability of financial evaluation measures to evaluate IT investments. These introductory questions will be taken up again in order to provide answers to them:

* Does a single evaluation measure exist that is generally "the best" for IT investment appraisal?
* Are financial performance measures capable of evaluating all aspects that arise from IT investments?
* Does evaluating IT investments only by financial performance measures prevent them from being carried out?
* How can one know if and when payoff from previous or future IT investments will be realized?

The answer to the first question is no. All researchers on this field, including the results of this work, agree that the complexity of IT investments and the characteristic features of financial evaluation measures make it impossible to find a single evaluation measure that masters all situations.

Concerning the second question, the results of the suitability analysis show that each examined financial evaluation measure has its advantages and disadvantages. There is no aspect of IT investments that is not regarded by any of the examined measures. However, assigning certain measures to certain circumstances is necessary, as illustrated in chapter 4.2. The only evaluation measure capable of taking all aspects of IT investments into account is Tobin's q, although most are only partly regarded. Nevertheless, Tobin's q is the most suitable evaluation measure, if an IT investment has a strategic value for the company, which is reflected by intangible benefits such as new-business opportunities, long-term benefits and organizational changes.

There is no yes or no answer possible to the third question. Under certain circumstances the answer is yes, e.g. if some measures are solely taken into consideration for decisions towards investment realizations, they can prevent profitable investments from being carried out. For instance, an in advance calculated NPV of a project can be negative and hence the project will be rejected. Calculating the same project with the real options analysis may provide a positive NPV. "Inappropriate use of DCF analysis results in the mistaken rejection of worthwhile long-term investment opportunities, thereby biasing the firm's investment decisions toward short-term profits"[179]. The answer to the third question is no, if the appropriate financial evaluation measure, or a combination of some of them, is chosen with regard to the individual characteristics or predetermined goals of the investment. This can be achieved by considering a decision-supporting framework.

The answer to the forth question, is that a structured proceeding at an IT investment project is necessary. One will know when payoff is realized, when the goals of the investment are set in advance and the chosen evaluation method is able to measure these goals. Setting goals should not be problematic as far as investments are undertaken out of an existing need and finding the appropriate evaluation method can be achieved by considering one of the available frameworks.

In general, the research in this field has not yet come to an end. New evaluation techniques and variations or combinations of already existing ones will be developed, which will prove to be more or less suitable. This work is limited to the analysis of *financial* evaluation measures and therefore does not raise a claim to judge all evaluation techniques for IT investment appraisal. It tries to give answers to some questions on the suitability of financial IT investment evaluation measures and basically the reader should bear in mind that "evaluation techniques are a tool to aid judgement and not a replacement of judgement"[180], as some researchers state.

---

[179] Kumaraswamy (1996), p. 2.
[180] King and Mcaulay (1997), p. 133.

Bibliography

Abel, A.B.; Eberly, J.C. (2003): Q Theory Without Adjustment Costs & Cash Flow Effects Without Financing Constraints. In: Society for Economic Dynamics, 2004 Meeting Papers, No. 205, http://finance.wharton.upenn.edu/~abel/pdf_files_papers/Cas hFlow-posted.pdf, access at 04-04-2005.

Alinean (2005a): Alinean Unveils ROIT: New Metric Linking IT Spending and Financial Performance, http://www.alinean.com/PR-Peer%20Comparison%20ROIT%20Final.asp, access at 03-16-2005.

Alinean (2005b): Return on IT (ROIT), http://www.alinean.com/Return%20on%20IT%20August%20 2004.pdf, access at 03-16-2005.

Baecker, P.N.; Hommel, U. (2003): 25 Years Real Options Approach to Investment Valuation: Review and Assessment. In: Zeitschrift für Betriebswirtschaft, Ergänzungsheft 3/2004, pp. 1-53.

Brach, M.A. (2003): Real Options in practise, Hoboken, New Jersey.

Broyles, J. (2003): Financial Management and Real Options, Chichester, West Sussex.

Brynjolfsson, E. (1993): The Productivity Paradox of Information Technology. In: Communications of the ACM, Vol. 36, No. 12, pp. 67-77.

Brynjolfsson, E.; Hitt, L.M. (1993): Paradox Lost? Firm-level Evidence of High Return to Informations Systems Spending. In: Management Science, Vol. 42, No. 4, 1998, pp. 541-558, http://ccs.mit.edu/papers/CCSWP162/CCSWP162.html, access at 02-17-2005.

Brynjolfsson, E.; Hitt, L.M. (1998): Beyond the Productivity Paradox: Computers are the Catalyst for Bigger Changes. In: Communications of the ACM, Vol. 41, No. 8, 1998, pp. 49-55.

Brynjolfsson, E.; Hitt, L.M. (2000): Beyond Computation: Information Technology, Organizational Transformation and Business Performance. In: Journal of Economic Perspectives, Vol. 14, No. 4, 2000, pp. 23-48.

Brynjolfsson, E.; Yang, S. (1996): Information Technology and Productivity: A Review of the Literature, Advances in Computers. In: Academic Press, Vol. 43, 1996, pp. 197-214.

Brynjolfsson, E.; Yang, S. (1999): The Intangible Costs and Benefits of Computer Investments: Evidence from the Financial Markets. In: Proceedings of the eighteenth international conference on Information Systems, Revised December 1999, pp. 1-52.

Copeland, T.; Tufano, P. (2004): A Real-World Way to Manage Real Options. In: Harvard Business Review, March 1, 2004, pp. 90-99.

Dehning, B.; Richardson, V.J. (2002): Returns on Investments in Information Technology: A Research Synthesis. In: Journal of Information Systems, Vol. 16, No. 1, Spring 2002, pp. 7-30.

Deloitte (2005): Summary of IAS 38, http://www.iasplus.com/standard/ias38.htm, access at 03-29-2005.

Devaraj, S.; Kohli, R. (2002): The IT Payoff: Measuring the Business Value of Information Technology Investments, Upper Saddle River NJ.

Dix, J. (2004): CIO's thoughts about evaluating techs, agility. In: Network World, 5/31/04, p. 32.

Drukarczyk, J. (2003): Unternehmensbewertung, München.

Ewert, R.; Wagenhofer, A. (2003): Interne Unternehmensrechnung, Berlin.

Farbey, B.; Land, F.F.; Targett, D. (1994): Matching and IT project with an appropriate method of evaluation: a research note on `Evaluating Investments in IT´. In: Journal of Information Technology, 1994, Vol. 9, pp. 239-243.

Franke, G.; Hax, H. (1999): Finanzwirtschaft des Unternehmens und Kapitalmarkt, 4th edition, Berlin.

Gartenberg, M. (2000, October 30): Myths beyond TCO. In: Computerworld, 34 (44), pp. 52-54.

Götze, U.; Glaser, K. (2001): Economic Value Added als Instrument einer wertorientierten Unternehmensführung: Methodik und anwendungsspezifische Beurteilung. In: krp-Sonderheft 1/2001, pp. 31- 37.

Gormely, J.; Bluestein W.; Gatoff J.; Chun H. (1998): The Runaway Costs of Packaged Applications. In: The Forrester Report, Vol. 3, No. 5, Forrester Research, Inc., Cambridge, MA. Cited in: Brynjolfsson, E.; Yang, S. (1997): The Intangible Costs and Benefits of Computer Investments: Evidence from the Financial Markets. In: Proceedings of the eighteenth international conference on Information Systems, Revised December 1999, pp. 1-52.

Grant, J.L. (1997): Foundations of Economic Value Added, New Hope.

Groh, G. (1997): Total Cost of Ownership - Diskussion und Anbieterpositionierung. In: Bullinger, H.J. (1997): TCO: Total Cost of Ownership. IAO-Forum, Stuttgart, 12-20-1997, pp. 39-56.

Hitt, L.M.; Brynjolfsson, E. (1994): Creating Value and Destroying Profits? Three Measures of Information Technology's contribution. In: MIT, Sloan Working Paper, December 1994, http://ccs.mit.edu/papers/CCSWP183.html, access at 11-23-2004.

Hopwood, A.; Leuz, C.; Pfaff, D. (2004): The Economics and Politics of Accounting: International Essays, Oxford University Press.

Howell, S.; Stark, A.; Newton, D.; Paxson, D.; Cavus, M.; Pereira, J.; Patel, K. (2001): Real Options: Evaluating Corporate Investments Opportunities in a Dynamic World, Financial Times: Prentice Hall.

Jeffery, M.; Shah, S.; Sweeney, R.J.(2003): Real Options And Enterprise Technology Project Selection And Deployment Strategies. In: MIS Quaterly, April 2003.

Johnston, B. (2004): Good to Great Shareholder Value from IT Investments, http://www.computerworld.com/managementtopics/manage ment/itspending/story/0,10801,96054,00.html, access at 03-16-2005.

Keen, J. (1995): The evaluation of leading-edge technologies. In: Hard Money - Soft Outcomes, Farbey, B.; Targett, D.; and Land, F. (eds) (Alfred Waller, Henrey), pp. 135-147.

Kelleher, J.C.; MacCormack, J.J. (2005): Internal rate of return: A cautionary tale. In: McKinsey Quaterly, 2005 Special Edition, pp. 70-76.

King, M.; Mcaulay, L. (1997): Information technology investment evaluation: evidence and interpretation. In: Journal of Information Technology, Vol. 12, 1997, pp. 131-143.

Kloock, J.; Coenen, M. (1996): Cash-Flow-Return on Investment als Rentabilitätskennzahl aus externer Sicht. In: Das Wirtschaftstudium, 25. Jg., 1996, pp. 1101-1107.

Kumaraswamy, A. (1996): A Real Options Perspective of Firm's R&D Investments. Ann Arbor, UMI, 1997.

Lee, K. (2001): ROI calculators help gauge benefit, turnover cots. In: Employee Benefit News, Vol. 15, Issue 14, November 2001, p. 11.

Lei, K.; Rawles, P.T. (2003): Strategic Decisions On Technology Selections for Facilitating A Network/Systems Laboratory Using Real Options & Total Cost of Ownership Theories. In: Proceeding of the 4th conference on information technology curriculum on Information Technology education, 2003, pp. 76-92.

Madden, B.J. (1999): CFROI Valuation: A Total System Approach to Valuing the Firm, Oxford.

Mengele, A. (1999): Shareholder-Return und Shareholder-Risk als unternehmensinterne Steuerungsgrößen, Stuttgart.

Miles, J.A.; Ezzell, J.R. (1980): The Weighted Average Cost of Capital, Perfect Capital Markets, and Project Life: A Clarification. In: Journal of Financial and Quantitative Analysis, Vol. 15, No. 3, September 1980, pp. 719-730.

Mogollon, M.; Raisinghani, M.S. (2004): Measuring ROI in E-Commerce Applications: Analysis to Action. In: Van Grembergen, W. (2004): Strategies for information Technology Governance, pp. 187-215.

Mun, J. (2003): Real Options Analysis Course: Business Cases and Software Applications, Hoboken, New Jersey.

Plesman Publications; Gale Group (2002): What about ROI? - Editorial - information technology investment costs In: http://www.findarticles.com/p/articles/mi_m0CGC/is_21_28/ai _93734798, access at 05-04-2005.

Powell, P. (1992): Information technology evaluation: is it different? In: Journal of the Operational Research Society. 43(1), 1992, pp. 29-42.

Rai, A.; Patnayakuni, R.; Patnayakuni, N. (1997): Technology Investment and Business Performance. In: Communications of the ACM, Vol. 40, No. 7, pp. 89-97.

Rappaport, A. (1998): Creating Shareholder Value: a guide for managers and investors, New York.

Riverbank, W.C.; FitzGerald, K.M.; Schelin, S.H.; Yates, W.H.; Runkle, T. (2001): Information Technology Investments - Metrics for Business Decisions, Center for Public Technology,

Institute of Government, The University of North Carolina at Chapel Hill, http://www.cpt.unc.edu/pdfs/Final%20Report.pdf , access at 03-09-2005.

Schwarze, J. (2000): Einführung in die Wirtschaftsinformatik, 5th revised edition, Herne/Berlin.

Selchert, M. (2004): Ermittlung des Erfolgs von CRM-Systemen: Konzeption und praktische Anwendung. In: Controlling, 1st Vol., January 2004, pp. 27-34.

Smith David, J.; Schuff, D.; St. Louis, R. (2002): Managing Your IT Total Cost of Ownership. In: Communications of the ACM, Vol. 45, No. 1, 2002, pp. 101-106.

Stahlknecht, P.; Hasenkamp, U.; (2002): Einführung in die Wirt-schaftsinformatik, 10th revised edition, Berlin, Heidelberg, New York.

Stern Stewart & Co. (2005): About EVA, http://www.sternstewart.com/evaabout/whatis.php, access at 03-05-2005.

Value Based Management.net (2005): Internal Rate of Return – IRR. http://www.valuebasedmanagement.net/methods_irr.html, access at 5-13-2005.

Van der Zee, H. (2002): Measuring the Value of Information Technology, Hershey, London.

Van Grembergen, W. (2001): Information Technology Evaluation Methods and Management, Hershey, London.

Villalonga, B. (2000): Intangible resources, Tobin's q, and sus-tainability of performance differences. In: Journal of Economic Behaviour & Organization, Vol. 54, 2004, pp. 205-230.